SIDE by SIDE

THIRD EDITION

BOOK 1B

Steven J. Molinsky
Bill Bliss

Illustrated by

Richard E. Hill

Longman

CONTENTS

Side by Side, 3rd edition
Student Book/Workbook 1B

Copyright © 2001 by Prentice Hall Regents
Addison Wesley Longman, Inc.
A Pearson Education Company.
All rights reserved.
No part of this publication may be reproduced, stored in a retrieval system, or transmitted in any form or by any means, electronic, mechanical, photocopying, recording, or otherwise, without the prior permission of the publisher.

Pearson Education, 10 Bank Street, White Plains, NY 10606

Vice president, director of publishing: *Allen Ascher*
Editorial manager: *Pam Fishman*
Vice president, director of design and production: *Rhea Banker*
Associate director of electronic production: *Aliza Greenblatt*
Production manager: *Ray Keating*

Director of manufacturing: *Patrice Fraccio*
Digital layout specialist: *Wendy Wolf, Paula Williams*
Associate art director: *Elizabeth Carlson*
Interior design: *Elizabeth Carlson, Wendy Wolf*
Cover design: *Elizabeth Carlson*
Copyediting: *Janet Johnston*

Contributing *Side by Side* Gazette authors: *Laura English, Meredith Westfall*

Photo credits: p. 98 (*top*) Randi Anglin/The Image Works, (*second from top*) David S. Robbins/Tony Stone Images, NY, (*second from bottom*) Richemond/The Image Works, (*bottom*) Tony Stone Images, NY; p. 115, Starr/Stock Boston; p. 116, (*top left*) Topham/The Image Works, (*botom, left*) Paolo Negri/Tony Stone Images, NY, (*center*) G. Salomone, Granata Press/The Image Works, (*right*) T & D McCarthy/The Stock Market; p. 140, (*top*) John Coletti/Stock Boston, (*center*) Index Stock Photography,

(*bottom*) David Simson/Stock Boston; p. 165, (*bottom, right*) Eric Sander/Liaison Agency, Inc., (*top*) Jeff Greenberg/The Image Works, (*bottom, left*) Lee Snider/The Image Works; p. 166, (*top, left*) Jeff Greenberg/The Image Works, (*top, center*) Owen Franken/Corbis, (*top, right*) David Young-Wolff/Tony Stone Images, NY, (*bottom, left*) Frank Siteman/Omni-Photo Communications, Inc., (*bottom, center*) Willie L. Hill/The Image Works, (*bottom, right*) David Young-Wolff/PhotoEdit.

The authors gratefully acknowledge the contribution of Tina Carver in the development of the original *Side by Side* program.

ISBN 0-13-029290-7

15 16 – V082 – 14 13 12 11

Printed in the United States of America

Simple Present Tense

- Languages and Nationalities
- Everyday Activities

VOCABULARY PREVIEW

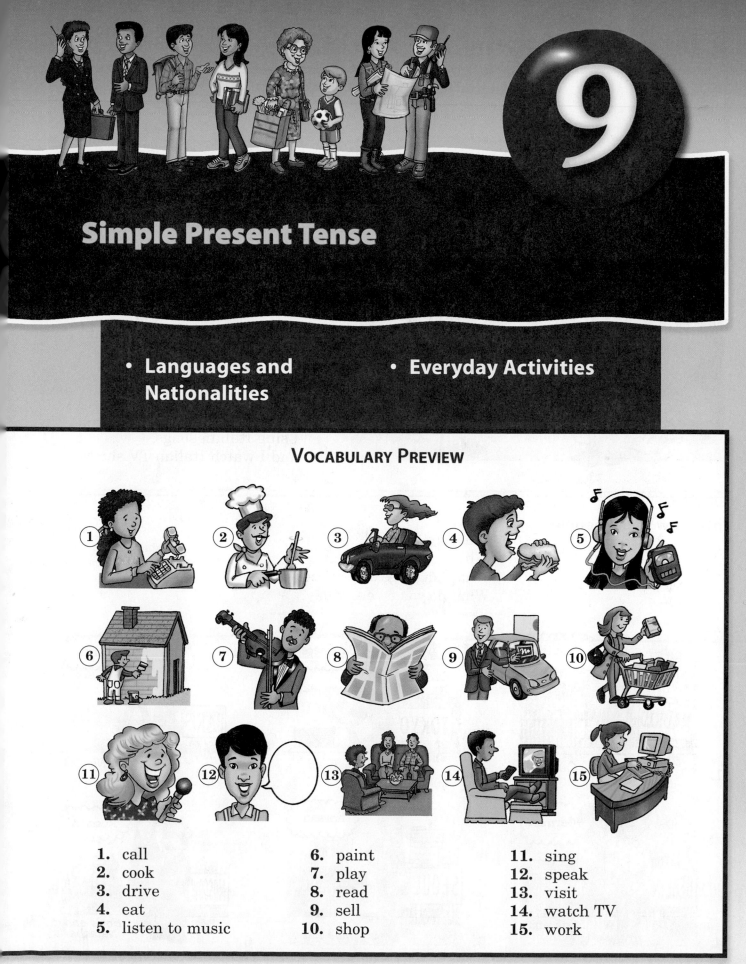

1. call
2. cook
3. drive
4. eat
5. listen to music
6. paint
7. play
8. read
9. sell
10. shop
11. sing
12. speak
13. visit
14. watch TV
15. work

Interviews Around the World

| I We You They | live. | Where do { I we you they } live? | What do { I we you they } do? |

A. What's your name?

B. My name is Antonio.

A. Where do you live?

B. I live in Rome.

A. What language do you speak?

B. I speak Italian.

A. Tell me, what do you do every day?

B. I eat Italian food,
   I sing Italian songs,
   and I watch Italian TV shows!

Interview these people.

What's your name?
Where do you live?
What language do you speak?
What do you do every day?

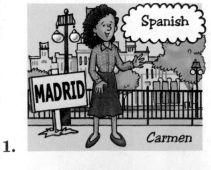

1. Carmen — Spanish — MADRID

2. Kenji — Japanese — TOKYO

3. Nicole — French — PARIS

4. Erik and Monika — German — BERLIN

5. Jae Hee — Korean — SEOUL

6. Boris and Natasha — Russian — MOSCOW

People Around the World

He She It } lives.	Where does { he she it } live?	What does { he she it } do?

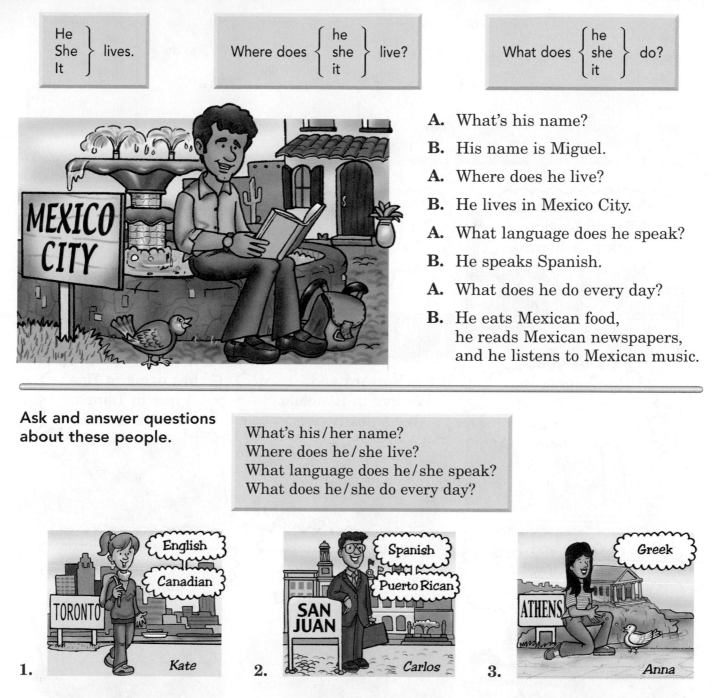

A. What's his name?

B. His name is Miguel.

A. Where does he live?

B. He lives in Mexico City.

A. What language does he speak?

B. He speaks Spanish.

A. What does he do every day?

B. He eats Mexican food,
he reads Mexican newspapers,
and he listens to Mexican music.

Ask and answer questions about these people.

What's his/her name?
Where does he/she live?
What language does he/she speak?
What does he/she do every day?

1. Kate — English, Canadian, TORONTO

2. Carlos — Spanish, Puerto Rican, SAN JUAN

3. Anna — Greek, ATHENS

4. Ming — Chinese, HONG KONG

5. Sonia — Portuguese, Brazilian, RIO de JANEIRO

6. Omar — Arabic, Egyptian, CAIRO

81

TALK ABOUT IT! *Where Do They Live, and What Do They Do?*

Use these models to talk with other students about the people above.

A. Where does *Linda* live?

B. *She* lives in *London.*

A. What does *she* do?

B. *She works in a library.*

A. Where do *Walter* and *Wendy* live?

B. They live in *Washington, D.C.*

A. What do they do?

B. They *work in an office.*

How About You?

Where do you live? What do you do?

MR. AND MRS. DiCARLO

Mr. and Mrs. DiCarlo live in an old Italian neighborhood in New York City. They speak a little English, but usually they speak Italian.

They read the Italian newspaper. They listen to Italian radio programs. They shop at the Italian grocery store around the corner from their apartment building. And every day they visit their friends and neighbors and talk about life back in "the old country."

Mr. and Mrs. DiCarlo are upset about their son, Joe. He lives in a small suburb outside the city. He speaks a little Italian, but usually he speaks English. He reads American newspapers. He listens to American radio programs. He shops at big suburban supermarkets and shopping malls. And when he visits his friends and neighbors, he always speaks English.

In fact, Joe speaks Italian only when he calls his parents on the telephone, or when he visits them every weekend.

Mr. and Mrs. DiCarlo are sad because their son speaks so little Italian. They're afraid he's forgetting his language, his culture, and his country.

✔ READING CHECK-UP

WHAT'S THE ANSWER?

1. Where do Mr. and Mrs. DiCarlo live?
2. Where does Joe live?
3. What language do Mr. and Mrs. DiCarlo usually speak?
4. What language does Joe usually speak?
5. What do Mr. and Mrs. DiCarlo read?
6. What does Joe read?

7. What do Mr. and Mrs. DiCarlo listen to?
8. What does Joe listen to?
9. Where do Mr. and Mrs. DiCarlo shop?
10. Where does Joe shop?

WHICH WORD IS CORRECT?

1. Mrs. DiCarlo (read   reads) the Italian newspaper.
2. Mr. DiCarlo (shop   shops) at the Italian grocery store.
3. They (live   lives) in New York City.
4. Joe (live   lives) outside the city.
5. He (speak   speaks) English.
6. Mr. and Mrs. DiCarlo (listen   listens) to the radio.
7. They (visit   visits) their friends every day.
8. Their friends (talk   talks) about life back in "the old country."
9. Joe (call   calls) his parents on the telephone.
10. Joe's friends (speak   speaks) English.

LISTENING

Listen and choose the correct answer.

1. a. live   b. lives
2. a. work   b. works
3. a. speak   b. speaks
4. a. drive   b. drives
5. a. read   b. reads

6. a. visit   b. visits
7. a. cook   b. cooks
8. a. paint   b. paints
9. a. call   b. calls
10. a. shop   b. shops

How to Say It!

Hesitating

A. What do you do every day?
B. Hmm. Well . . .
   I *work*, I *read the newspaper*, and I *visit my friends*.

Practice conversations with other students. Hesitate while you're thinking of your answer.

IN YOUR OWN WORDS

MRS. KOWALSKI

Mrs. Kowalski lives in an old Polish neighborhood in Chicago. She's upset about her son, Michael, and his wife, Kathy. Using the story on page 83 as a model, tell a story about Mrs. Kowalski.

INTERVIEW

Where do you live?
What language do you speak?
What do you do every day?

Interview another student.

Then tell the class about that person.

I live in an apartment in the city.
I speak Spanish and a little English.
I go to school and visit my friends.

She lives in an apartment in the city.
She speaks Spanish and a little English.
She goes to school and visits her friends.

Listen. Then say it.

Where does he work?

Where does she live?

What does he do?

What does she read?

Say it. Then listen.

Where does he shop?

Where does she eat?

What does he cook?

What does she talk about?

Where do you live? What language do you speak? What do you do every day? Write a paragraph about it in your journal.

CHAPTER SUMMARY

GRAMMAR

SIMPLE PRESENT TENSE

Where	do	I we you they	live?
	does	he she it	

I We You They	live	in Rome.
He She It	lives	

KEY VOCABULARY

EVERYDAY ACTIVITIES		NATIONALITIES	LANGUAGES	NATIONALITIES	LANGUAGES
call	sell	Brazilian	Portuguese	Japanese	Japanese
cook	shop	Canadian	English, French	Korean	Korean
drive	sing	Chinese	Chinese	Mexican	Spanish
eat	speak	Egyptian	Arabic	Polish	Polish
listen	visit	French	French	Puerto Rican	Spanish
paint	watch TV	German	German	Russian	Russian
play	work	Greek	Greek	Spanish	Spanish
read		Italian	Italian		

10

Simple Present Tense:
Yes/No Questions
Negatives
Short Answers

- **Habitual Actions**
- **People's Interests and Activities**

Vocabulary Preview

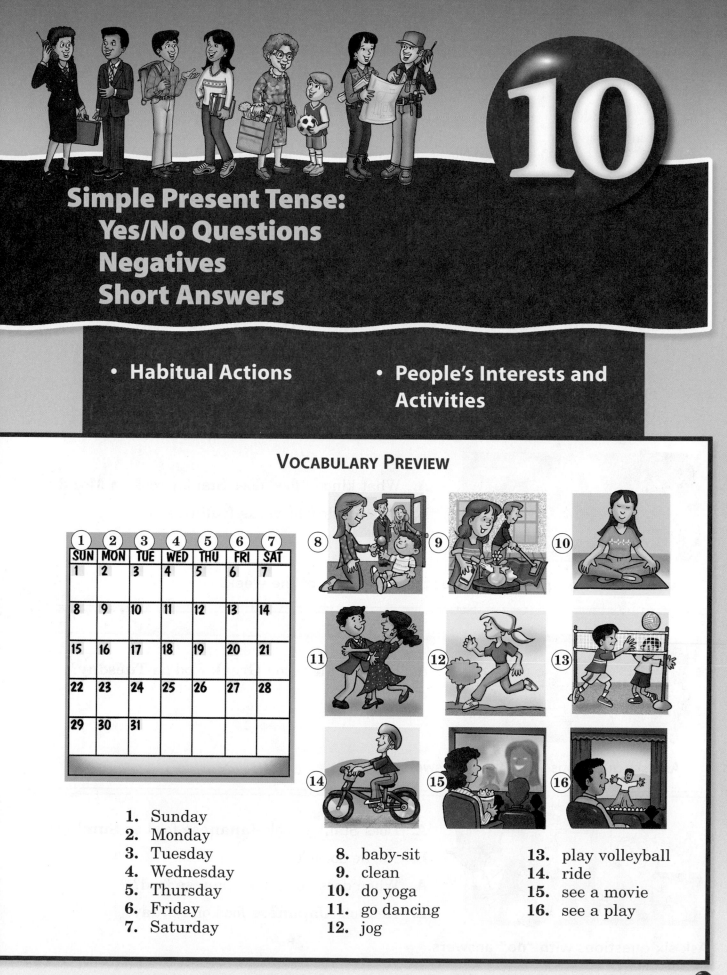

1. Sunday
2. Monday
3. Tuesday
4. Wednesday
5. Thursday
6. Friday
7. Saturday

8. baby-sit
9. clean
10. do yoga
11. go dancing
12. jog

13. play volleyball
14. ride
15. see a movie
16. see a play

Stanley's International Restaurant

He cooks.	Does he cook?	What kind of food ⎫ does he cook?
He doesn't cook.	Yes, he does.	When ⎭
(does not)	No, he doesn't.	

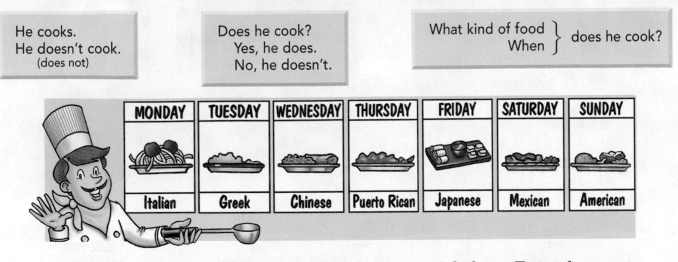

MONDAY	TUESDAY	WEDNESDAY	THURSDAY	FRIDAY	SATURDAY	SUNDAY
Italian	Greek	Chinese	Puerto Rican	Japanese	Mexican	American

Stanley's International Restaurant is a very special place. Every day Stanley cooks a different kind of food. On Monday he cooks Italian food. On Tuesday he cooks Greek food. On Wednesday he cooks Chinese food. On Thursday he cooks Puerto Rican food. On Friday he cooks Japanese food. On Saturday he cooks Mexican food. And on Sunday he cooks American food.

A. What kind of food does Stanley cook on **Monday**?

B. On **Monday** he cooks **Italian** food.

Ask and answer questions about the other days of the week.

A. Does Stanley cook **Greek** food on **Tuesday**?

B. Yes, he does.

Ask six questions with "yes" answers.

A. Does Stanley cook **Japanese** food on **Sunday**?

B. No, he doesn't.

A. When does he cook **Japanese** food?

B. He cooks **Japanese** food on **Friday**.

Ask six questions with "no" answers.

You go.	Do you go?	
You don't go.	Yes, I do. / Yes, we do.	When do you go?
(do not)	No, I don't. / No, we don't.	

A. Do you go to Stanley's Restaurant on **Wednesday**?

B. Yes, I do.

A. Why?

B. Because I like **Chinese** food.

Ask these people.

1. *Monday?* 2. *Thursday?* 3. *Saturday?* 4. *Sunday?*

A. Do you go to Stanley's Restaurant on **Sunday**?

B. No, I don't.

A. Why not?

B. Because I don't like **American** food.

Ask these people.

5. *Tuesday?* 6. *Wednesday?* 7. *Friday?* 8. *Monday?*

A. What kind of food do you like?

B. I like **Russian** food.

A. When do you go to Stanley's Restaurant?

B. I don't go there.

A. Why not?

B. Because Stanley doesn't cook **Russian** food.

Ask these people.

9. *French* 10. *Ethiopian* 11. *Thai* 12. *Vietnamese*

Busy People!

| MONDAY | TUESDAY | WEDNESDAY | THURSDAY | FRIDAY | SATURDAY | SUNDAY |

Jeff is a very athletic person. He does a different kind of exercise or sport every day. On Monday he jogs. On Tuesday he plays tennis. On Wednesday he does yoga. On Thursday he swims. On Friday he goes to a health club. On Saturday he plays basketball. And on Sunday he rides his bike.

| MONDAY | TUESDAY | WEDNESDAY | THURSDAY | FRIDAY | SATURDAY | SUNDAY |

Julie is a very busy student. She does a different activity every day. On Monday she sings in the choir. On Tuesday she plays in the orchestra. On Wednesday she writes for the school newspaper. On Thursday she plays volleyball. On Friday she baby-sits for her neighbors. On Saturday she works at the mall. And on Sunday she visits her grandparents.

| MONDAY | TUESDAY | WEDNESDAY | THURSDAY | FRIDAY | SATURDAY | SUNDAY |

Mr. and Mrs. Baker are very active people. They do something different every day of the week. On Monday they go to a museum. On Tuesday they see a play. On Wednesday they go to a concert. On Thursday they take a karate lesson. On Friday they go dancing. On Saturday they see a movie. And on Sunday they play cards with their friends.

A. Does Jeff play tennis on Tuesday?

B. Yes, he does.

A. Does Julie work at the mall on Saturday?

B. Yes, she does.

A. Do Mr. and Mrs. Baker go dancing on Friday?

B. Yes, they do.

Ask other questions with "yes" answers.

A. Does Jeff do yoga on Sunday?

B. No, he doesn't.

A. Does Julie sing in the choir on Thursday?

B. No, she doesn't.

A. Do Mr. and Mrs. Baker see a movie on Monday?

B. No, they don't.

Ask other questions with "no" answers.

Now interview Jeff, Julie, and Mr. and Mrs. Baker. Practice conversations with other students.

91

EVERY WEEKEND IS IMPORTANT TO THE GARCIA FAMILY

Every weekend is important to the Garcia family. During the week they don't have very much time together, but they spend a LOT of time together on the weekend.

Mr. Garcia works at the post office during the week, but he doesn't work there on the weekend. Mrs. Garcia works at the bank during the week, but she doesn't work there on the weekend. Jennifer and Jonathan Garcia go to school during the week, but they don't go to school on the weekend. And the Garcias' dog, Max, stays home alone during the week, but he doesn't stay home alone on the weekend.

On Saturday and Sunday the Garcias spend time together. On Saturday morning they clean the house together. On Saturday afternoon they work in the garden together. And on Saturday evening they watch videos together. On Sunday morning they go to church together. On Sunday afternoon they have a big dinner together. And on Sunday evening they play their musical instruments together.

As you can see, every weekend is special to the Garcias. It's their only time together as a family.

✓ READING CHECK-UP

Q & A

Using these models, make questions and answers based on the story on page 92.

A. What *does Mr. Garcia* do during the week?

B. *He works at the post office.*

A. What do the Garcias do on *Saturday morning*?

B. They *clean the house* together.

DO OR DOES?

1. _____ Mr. Garcia work on the weekend?
2. _____ Jennifer and Jonathan go to school during the week?
3. When _____ they watch videos?
4. Where _____ Mrs. Garcia work?
5. _____ you speak Spanish?
6. What _____ Mr. Garcia do during the week?

WHAT'S THE ANSWER?

1. Does Mr. Garcia work at the post office?
2. Do Jennifer and Jonathan go to school during the week?
3. Does Mrs. Garcia work at the post office?
4. Do Mr. and Mrs. Garcia have much time together during the week?
5. Does Jennifer watch videos on Saturday evening?
6. Do Jennifer and her brother clean the house on Saturday morning?
7. Does Mr. Garcia work in the garden on Saturday evening?

DON'T OR DOESN'T?

1. Mr. and Mrs. Garcia _____ work on the weekend.
2. Jennifer _____ work at the bank.
3. We _____ watch videos during the week.
4. My son _____ play a musical instrument.
5. My sister and I _____ eat at Stanley's Restaurant.
6. Our dog _____ like our neighbor's dog.

LISTENING

WHAT'S THE WORD?

Listen and choose the word you hear.

1. a. do b. does
2. a. do b. does
3. a. Sunday b. Monday
4. a. don't b. doesn't
5. a. don't b. doesn't
6. a. does b. goes
7. a. Tuesday b. Thursday
8. a. go b. don't

WHAT'S THE ANSWER?

Listen and choose the correct response.

1. a. Yes, I do. b. Yes, he does.
2. a. Yes, they do. b. Yes, she does.
3. a. No, she doesn't. b. No, we don't.
4. a. No, he doesn't. b. No, we don't.
5. a. No, I don't. b. No, he doesn't.
6. a. No, I don't. b. No, they don't.
7. a. Yes, we do. b. Yes, they do.
8. a. Yes, they do. b. Yes, he does.

How About You?

Tell about yourself:
What do you do during the week?
What do you do on the weekend?

Now tell about another person—a friend, someone in your family, or another student:
What does he/she do during the week?
What does he/she do on the weekend?

93

READING

A VERY OUTGOING PERSON

Alice is a very outgoing person. She spends a lot of time with her friends. She goes to parties, she goes to movies, and she goes to concerts. She's very popular.

She also likes sports very much. She plays basketball, she plays baseball, and she plays volleyball. She's very athletic.

Alice doesn't stay home alone very often. She doesn't read many books, she doesn't watch TV, and she doesn't listen to music. She's very active.

As you can see, Alice is a very outgoing person.

IN YOUR OWN WORDS

For Writing and Discussion

A VERY SHY PERSON

Using the story about Alice as a model, tell a story about Sheldon. Begin your story:

Sheldon is a very shy person. He doesn't spend a lot of time with his friends. He doesn't go . . .

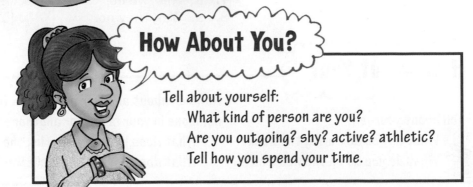

How About You?

Tell about yourself:
    What kind of person are you?
    Are you outgoing? shy? active? athletic?
    Tell how you spend your time.

How to Say It!

Starting a Conversation

A. Tell me, what kind of *movies* do you like?
B. I like *comedies.*
A. Who's your favorite *movie star*?
B. *Tim Kelly.*

Practice the interviews on this page, using "Tell me" to start the conversations.

INTERVIEW

First, answer these questions about yourself. Next, interview another student.
Then, tell the class about yourself and the other student.

1. **What kind of movies do you like?**

   Who's your favorite movie star?

   comedies   dramas   westerns   adventure movies   science fiction movies   cartoons

2. **What kind of books do you like?**

   Who's your favorite author?

   novels   poetry   short stories   non-fiction   biographies

3. **What kind of TV programs do you like?**

   Who's your favorite TV star?

   comedies   dramas   cartoons   game shows   news programs

4. **What kind of music do you like?**

   Who's your favorite performer?

   classical music   popular music   jazz   rock music   country music

5. **What kind of sports do you like?**

   Who's your favorite athlete? What's your favorite team?

   football   baseball   soccer   golf   hockey   tennis

PRONUNCIATION   Reduced *of*

Listen. Then say it.

What kind of movies do you like?

What kind of books do you like?

She spends a lot of time with her friends.

Say it. Then listen.

What kind of music do you like?

What kind of TV programs do you like?

I read a lot of books.

 SIDE by SIDE JOURNAL What do you do during the week? What do you do on the weekend? Write about it in your journal.

CHAPTER SUMMARY

GRAMMAR

SIMPLE PRESENT TENSE: YES/NO QUESTIONS

Do	I we you they	work?
Does	he she it	

SHORT ANSWERS

Yes,	I we you they	do.
	he she it	does.

No,	I we you they	don't.
	he she it	doesn't.

SIMPLE PRESENT TENSE: NEGATIVES

I We You They	don't	work.
He She It	doesn't	

KEY VOCABULARY

DAYS OF THE WEEK	NATIONALITIES	LANGUAGES	DESCRIBING PEOPLE	EVERYDAY ACTIVITIES	
Sunday	American	English	active	baby-sit	play volleyball
Monday	Chinese	Chinese	athletic	clean	ride a bicycle
Tuesday	Greek	Greek	busy	do yoga	see a movie
Wednesday	Italian	Italian	outgoing	go dancing	see a play
Thursday	Japanese	Japanese	popular	jog	
Friday	Mexican	Spanish	shy		
Saturday	Puerto Rican	Spanish			

 96

Volume 1   Number 4

Language

Millions speak Chinese. Only hundreds speak Bahinemo.

There are over 20,000 languages in the world. Some of these languages are very common. For example, millions of people speak Chinese, Spanish, English, Arabic, Portuguese, and Japanese. On the other hand, some languages are very rare. For example, only 500 people in Papua, New Guinea speak the language Bahinemo.

Languages grow and change. They borrow words from other languages. For example, in the English language, the word *rodeo* is from Spanish, *cafe* comes from French, *ketchup* is from Chinese, *sofa* is from Arabic, and *potato* comes from Haitian Kreyol. New words also come from technology. For example, *cyberspace*, *website*, and *e-mail* are recent words that relate to the Internet.

FACT FILE

Common Languages

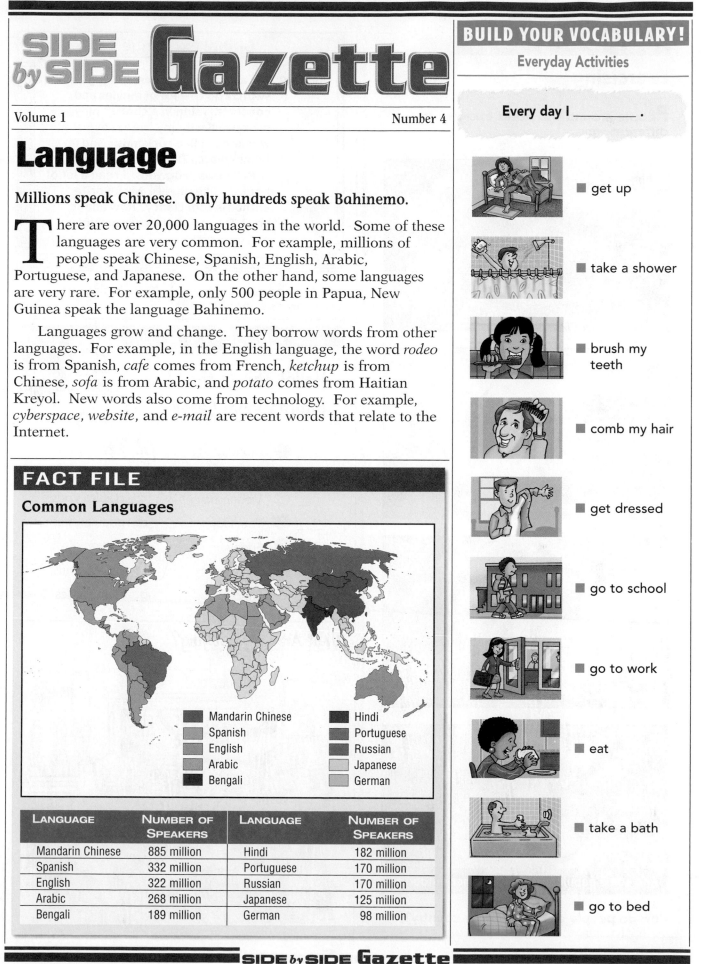

Legend	
Mandarin Chinese	Hindi
Spanish	Portuguese
English	Russian
Arabic	Japanese
Bengali	German

LANGUAGE	NUMBER OF SPEAKERS	LANGUAGE	NUMBER OF SPEAKERS
Mandarin Chinese	885 million	Hindi	182 million
Spanish	332 million	Portuguese	170 million
English	322 million	Russian	170 million
Arabic	268 million	Japanese	125 million
Bengali	189 million	German	98 million

BUILD YOUR VOCABULARY!

Everyday Activities

Every day I _____ .

- get up
- take a shower
- brush my teeth
- comb my hair
- get dressed
- go to school
- go to work
- eat
- take a bath
- go to bed

AROUND THE WORLD

Exercising

People around the world exercise in different ways.

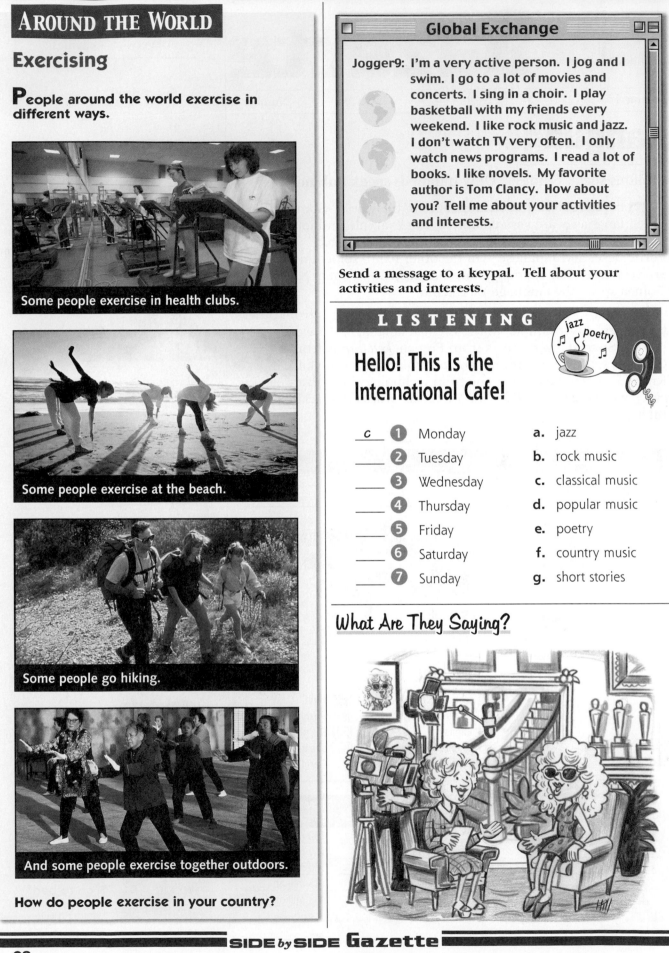

Some people exercise in health clubs.

Some people exercise at the beach.

Some people go hiking.

And some people exercise together outdoors.

How do people exercise in your country?

Global Exchange

Jogger9: I'm a very active person. I jog and I swim. I go to a lot of movies and concerts. I sing in a choir. I play basketball with my friends every weekend. I like rock music and jazz. I don't watch TV very often. I only watch news programs. I read a lot of books. I like novels. My favorite author is Tom Clancy. How about you? Tell me about your activities and interests.

Send a message to a keypal. Tell about your activities and interests.

LISTENING

jazz poetry

Hello! This Is the International Cafe!

_c_ ❶ Monday   **a.** jazz

❷ Tuesday   **b.** rock music

❸ Wednesday   **c.** classical music

❹ Thursday   **d.** popular music

❺ Friday   **e.** poetry

❻ Saturday   **f.** country music

❼ Sunday   **g.** short stories

What Are They Saying?

Object Pronouns
Simple Present Tense: *-s* vs. non-*s* Endings
Have/Has
Adverbs of Frequency

- **Describing Frequency of Actions**
- **Describing People**

VOCABULARY PREVIEW

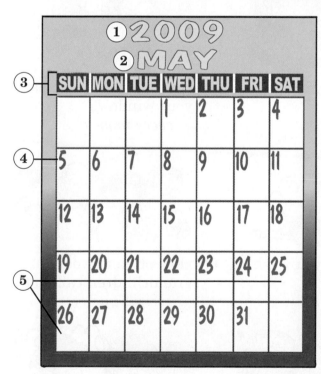

1. year
2. month
3. week
4. day
5. weekend

6. morning
7. afternoon
8. evening
9. night

How Often?

I	me
he	him
she	her
it	it
we	us
you	you
they	them

A. How often does your boyfriend call you?

B. He calls me every night.

1. How often do you use your computer?
every day

2. How often do you write to your son?
every week

3. How often do you clean your windows?
every month

4. How often do you visit your aunt in Minnesota?
every year

5. How often do you wash your car?
every weekend

6. How often do your grandchildren call you?
every Sunday

7. How often does your boss say "hello" to you?
every morning

8. How often do you feed the animals?
every afternoon

9. How often do you think about me?
all the time

She Usually Studies in the Library

[s]		[z]		[ɪz]			
eat	eats	read	reads	wash	washes	always	100%
write	writes	jog	jogs	watch	watches	usually	90%
bark	barks	call	calls	dance	dances	sometimes	50%
speak	speaks	clean	cleans	fix	fixes	rarely	10%
						never	0%

A. Does Carmen usually study in her room?

B. No. She rarely studies in her room.
She usually studies in the library.

1. Does Linda usually eat lunch in her office?
rarely
in the cafeteria

2. Does Alan always watch the news after dinner?
never
game shows

3. Does Diane sometimes read *The National Star*?
never
Time magazine

4. Does Henry usually wash his car on Sunday?
rarely
on Saturday

5. Does your girlfriend usually jog in the evening?
sometimes
in the afternoon

6. Does your neighbor's dog always bark during the day?
never
at night

We Have Noisy Neighbors

I		
We	have	
You		
They		brown eyes.
He		
She	has	
It		

A. Do you have quiet neighbors?

B. No. We have noisy neighbors.

1. Do you have a sister?
a brother

2. Does this store have an elevator?
an escalator

3. Does your daughter have straight hair?
curly hair

4. Does your son have brown hair?
blond hair

5. Do you and your husband have a dog?
a cat

6. Does your baby boy have blue eyes?
brown eyes

7. Do Mr. and Mrs. Hill have a satellite dish?
an old TV antenna

8. Does your grandmother have a car?
a motorcycle

9.

My brother and I look very different. I have brown eyes and he has blue eyes. We both have brown hair, but I have short, curly hair and he has long, straight hair. I'm tall and thin. He's short and heavy.

As you can see, I don't look like my brother. We look very different.

Who in your family do you look like? Who DON'T you look like? Tell about it.

My sister and I are very different. I'm a teacher. She's a journalist. I live in Miami. She lives in London. I have a large house in the suburbs. She has a small apartment in the city.

I'm married. She's single. I play golf. She plays tennis. I play the piano. She doesn't play a musical instrument. On the weekend I usually watch videos and rarely go out. She never watches videos and always goes to parties.

As you can see, we're very different. But we're sisters . . . and we're friends.

Compare yourself with a member of your family, another student in your class, or a famous person. Tell how you and this person are different.

How to Say It!

Reacting to Information

A. Tell me about *your sister.*
B. *She's a journalist. She lives in London.*
A. Oh, really? That's interesting.

Practice conversations with other students. Talk about people you know.

CLOSE FRIENDS

My husband and I are very lucky. We have many close friends in this city, and they're all interesting people.

Our friend Greta is an actress. We see her when she isn't making a movie in Hollywood. When we get together with her, she always tells us about her life in Hollywood as a movie star. Greta is a very close friend. We like her very much.

Our friend Dan is a scientist. We see him when he isn't busy in his laboratory. When we get together with him, he always tells us about his new experiments. Dan is a very close friend. We like him very much.

Our friends Bob and Carol are famous television news reporters. We see them when they aren't traveling around the world. When we get together with them, they always tell us about their conversations with presidents and prime ministers. Bob and Carol are very close friends. We like them very much.

Unfortunately, we don't see Greta, Dan, Bob, or Carol very often. In fact, we rarely see them because they're usually so busy. But we think about them all the time.

✔ READING CHECK-UP

What's the Word?

Greta is a famous actress. _____**1** lives in Hollywood. _____**2** movies are very popular. When _____**3** walks down the street, people always say "hello" to _____**4** and tell _____**5** how much they like _____**6** movies.

Dan is always busy. _____**7** works in _____**8** laboratory every day. Dan's friends rarely see _____**9**. When they see _____**10**, _____**11** usually talks about _____**12** experiments. Everybody likes _____**13** very much. _____**14** is a very nice person.

Bob and Carol are television news reporters. _____**15** friends don't see _____**16** very often because _____**17** travel around the world all the time. Presidents and prime ministers often call _____**18** on the telephone. _____**19** like _____**20** work very much.

LISTENING

Listen to the conversations. Who and what are they talking about?

1. a. grandfather
   b. grandmother
2. a. window
   b. windows
3. a. brother
   b. sister

4. a. sink
   b. cars
5. a. neighbor
   b. neighbors
6. a. computer
   b. news reporter

7. a. game show
   b. car
8. a. Ms. Brown
   b. Mr. Wong
9. a. Ken
   b. Jim and Karen

IN YOUR OWN WORDS

For Writing and Discussion

MY CLOSE FRIENDS

Tell about your close friends.

What are their names?
Where do they live?
What do they do?
When do you get together with them?
What do you talk about?

PRONUNCIATION   Deleted *h*

Listen. Then say it.

I visit her every year.

I write to him every week.

We see her very often.

She calls him every month.

Say it. Then listen.

I visit him every year.

I write to her every week.

We see him very often.

He calls her every month.

Write in your journal about your daily activities.

I always _____.

I usually _____.   I sometimes _____.

I rarely _____.   I never _____.

CHAPTER SUMMARY

GRAMMAR

OBJECT PRONOUNS

He calls	me him her it us you them	every night.

HAVE/HAS

I We You They	have	
He She It	has	brown eyes.

SIMPLE PRESENT TENSE: *S* VS. NON-*S* ENDINGS

He She It	eats. reads. washes.	[s] [z] [ɪz]

I We You They	eat. read. wash.

ADVERBS OF FREQUENCY

I	always usually sometimes rarely never	wash my car.

KEY VOCABULARY

TIME EXPRESSIONS

day	morning
week	afternoon
month	evening
year	night
weekend	

DESCRIBING APPEARANCE

long hair	blond hair	brown eyes
short hair	brown hair	blue eyes
straight hair	black hair	
curly hair		

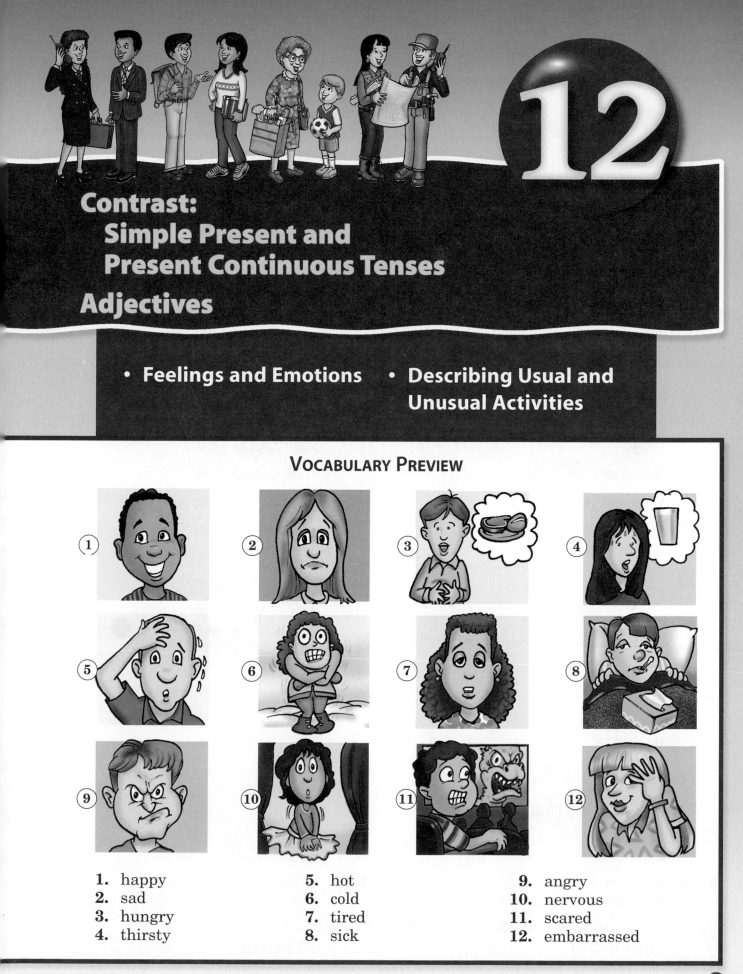

Contrast:
Simple Present and Present Continuous Tenses
Adjectives

- Feelings and Emotions
- Describing Usual and Unusual Activities

VOCABULARY PREVIEW

1. happy
2. sad
3. hungry
4. thirsty
5. hot
6. cold
7. tired
8. sick
9. angry
10. nervous
11. scared
12. embarrassed

I Always Cry When I'm Sad

cry
crying

A. Why are you crying?

B. I'm crying because I'm sad.
I ALWAYS cry when I'm sad.

smile
smiling

A. Why is she smiling?

B. She's smiling because she's happy.
She ALWAYS smiles when she's happy.

---

shout
shouting

1. A. Why are you shouting?

   B. _____ angry.

   I ALWAYS _____.

bite
biting

2. A. Why is he biting his nails?

   B. _____ nervous.

   He ALWAYS _____.

drink
drinking

3. A. Why is the bird drinking?

   B. _____ thirsty.

   It ALWAYS _____.

shiver
shivering

4. A. Why are they shivering?

   B. _____ cold.

   They ALWAYS _____.

go
going

5. A. Why are they going to
Stanley's Restaurant?

   B. _____ hungry.

   They ALWAYS _____.

go
going

6. A. Why is she going to
the doctor?

   B. _____ sick.

   She ALWAYS _____.

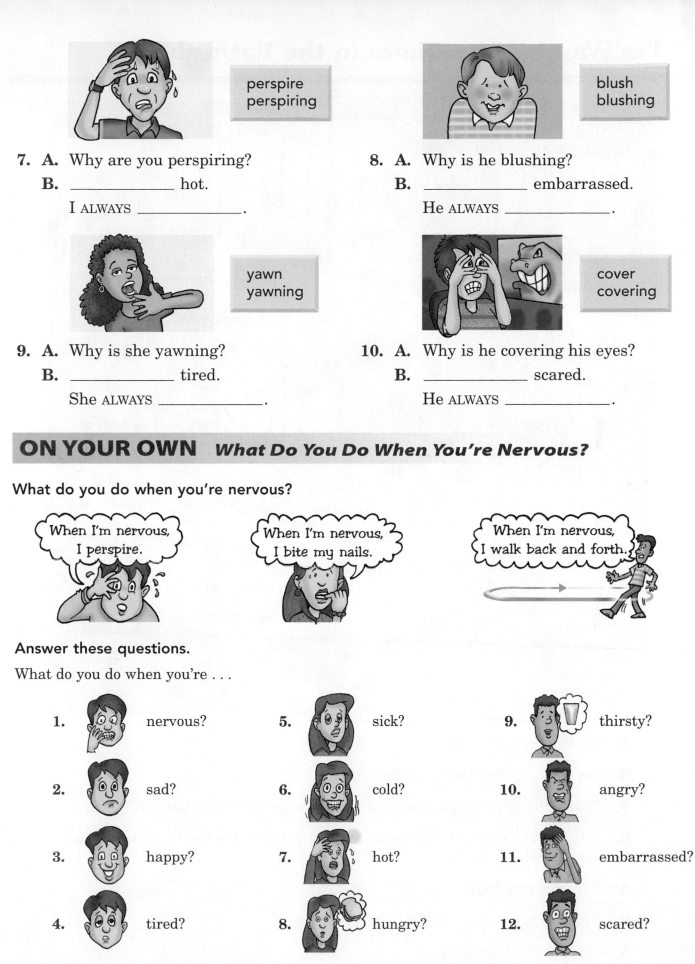

7. A. Why are you perspiring?
　　B. _____ hot.
　　　I ALWAYS _____ .

8. A. Why is he blushing?
　　B. _____ embarrassed.
　　　He ALWAYS _____ .

9. A. Why is she yawning?
　　B. _____ tired.
　　　She ALWAYS _____ .

10. A. Why is he covering his eyes?
　　B. _____ scared.
　　　He ALWAYS _____ .

ON YOUR OWN   *What Do You Do When You're Nervous?*

What do you do when you're nervous?

When I'm nervous, I perspire.

When I'm nervous, I bite my nails.

When I'm nervous, I walk back and forth.

Answer these questions.

What do you do when you're . . .

1. nervous?
2. sad?
3. happy?
4. tired?

5. sick?
6. cold?
7. hot?
8. hungry?

9. thirsty?
10. angry?
11. embarrassed?
12. scared?

Now ask another student in your class.

I'm Washing the Dishes in the Bathtub

A. What are you doing?!

B. I'm washing the dishes in the bathtub.

A. That's strange! Do you USUALLY wash the dishes in the bathtub?

B. No. I NEVER wash the dishes in the bathtub, but I'm washing the dishes in the bathtub TODAY.

A. Why are you doing THAT?!

B. Because my sink is broken.

A. I'm sorry to hear that.

A. What are you doing?!

B. I'm _____.

A. That's strange! Do you USUALLY _____?

B. No. I NEVER _____, but I'm _____ TODAY.

A. Why are you doing THAT?!

B. Because my _____ is broken.

A. I'm sorry to hear that.

1. *sleep*
   sleeping } *on the floor*
   bed

2. *study*
   studying } *with a flashlight*
   lamp

3. *walk*
   walking } *to work*
   car

4. *use*
   using } *a typewriter*
   computer

5. *sweep*
   sweeping } *the carpet*
   vacuum

6.

How to Say It!

Reacting to Bad News

A. *My sink is broken.*

B. { I'm sorry to hear that.
That's too bad!
What a shame!

Practice conversations with other students. Share some bad news and react to it.

READING

A BAD DAY AT THE OFFICE

Mr. Blaine is the president of the Acme Internet Company. The company has a staff of energetic employees. Unfortunately, all of the employees are out today. Nobody is there. As a result, Mr. Blaine is doing everybody's job, and he's having a VERY bad day at the office!

He's answering the telephone because the receptionist who usually answers it is at the dentist's office. He's typing letters because the secretary who usually types them is at home in bed with the flu. He's sorting the mail because the office assistant who usually sorts it is on vacation. And he's even cleaning the office because the custodian who usually cleans it is on strike.

Poor Mr. Blaine! It's a very busy day at the Acme Internet Company, and nobody is there to help him. He's having a VERY bad day at the office!

READING *CHECK-UP*

TRUE OR FALSE?

1. Mr. Blaine is the president of the Ajax Internet Company.
2. Mr. Blaine is out today.
3. The secretary is sick.

4. The office assistant is on strike.
5. The custodian isn't cleaning the office today.
6. The receptionist usually answers the phone at the dentist's office.

LISTENING

Listen and choose the correct answer.

1. a. I clean my house.
   b. I'm cleaning my house.
2. a. He sorts the mail.
   b. He's sorting the mail.
3. a. She answers the telephone.
   b. She's answering the telephone.

4. a. Yes. He yawns.
   b. Yes. He's yawning.
5. a. I'm covering my eyes.
   b. I cover my eyes.
6. a. I study in the library.
   b. I'm studying in the library.

EARLY MONDAY MORNING IN CENTERVILLE

Early Monday morning is usually a very busy time in Centerville. Men and women usually rush to their jobs. Some people walk to work, some people drive, and others take the bus. Children usually go to school. Some children walk to school, some children take the school bus, and others ride their bicycles. The city is usually very busy. Trucks deliver food to supermarkets, mail carriers deliver mail to homes and businesses, and police officers direct traffic at every corner. Yes, early Monday morning is usually a very busy time in Centerville.

✔ READING *CHECK-UP*

Using the story above as a guide, complete the following:

THE SNOWSTORM

Today isn't a typical early Monday morning in Centerville. In fact, it's a very unusual morning. It's snowing very hard there. All the people are at home. The streets are empty, and the city is quiet. The men and women who usually rush to their jobs aren't rushing to their jobs today. The people who usually walk to work aren't walking, the people who usually drive aren't _____¹, and the people who usually take the bus aren't _____² the bus. The children who usually go to school aren't _____³ to school today. The children who usually walk to school aren't _____⁴ today. The children who usually _____⁵ the school bus aren't _____⁶ it today. And the children who usually _____⁷ their bicycles aren't _____⁸ them this morning.

The city is very quiet. The trucks that usually _____⁹ food aren't _____¹⁰ it today. The mail carriers who usually _____¹¹ mail aren't _____¹² it this morning. And the police officers who usually _____¹³ traffic aren't _____¹⁴ it today. Yes, it's a very unusual Monday morning in Centerville.

Listen. Then say it.

I'm sorry to hear that.

We go to school.

He listens to the radio.

Mail carriers deliver mail to homes.

Say it. Then listen.

I'm happy to hear that.

They're going to the doctor.

She listens to music.

Trucks deliver food to supermarkets.

SIDE by SIDE JOURNAL

Describe a typical day in your city or town. What do people usually do? Write about it in your journal.

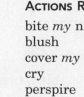

CHAPTER SUMMARY

GRAMMAR

SIMPLE PRESENT TENSE

> I always **cry** when I'm sad.
>
> I never **wash** the dishes in the bathtub.

PRESENT CONTINUOUS TENSE

> I'm **crying** because I'm sad.
>
> I'm **washing** the dishes in the bathtub today.

KEY VOCABULARY

FEELINGS AND EMOTIONS		ACTIONS RELATED TO FEELINGS AND EMOTIONS		EVERYDAY ACTIVITIES	
angry	nervous	bite *my* nails	shiver	clean	sweep
cold	sad	blush	shout	deliver	take the bus
embarrassed	scared	cover *my* eyes	smile	drive	type
happy	sick	cry	walk back and forth	ride a bicycle	use
hot	thirsty	perspire	yawn	sleep	walk
hungry	tired			study	wash

Volume 1   Number 5

Traffic: A Global Problem

There are more and more people and more and more cars

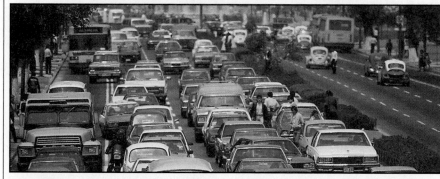

Traffic is a big problem in many cities around the world. Traffic is especially bad during *rush hour*—the time when people go to work or school and the time when they go home. Many people take buses, subways, or trains to work, but many other people drive their cars. As a result, the streets are very busy, and traffic is very bad.

Many cities are trying to solve their traffic problems. Some cities are building more roads. Other cities are expanding their bus and subway systems.

Many cities are trying to reduce the number of cars on their roads. Some highways have *carpool lanes*—special lanes for cars with two, three, or more people. In some cities, people drive their cars only on certain days of the week. For example, in Athens, people with license plate numbers ending in 0 through 4 drive on some days, and people with numbers ending in 5 through 9 drive on other days.

Every day around the world, more and more people drive to and from work in more and more cars. As a result, traffic is a global problem.

LISTENING

And Now, Here's Today's News!

TODAY'S NEWS

_b_ ① There's a subway problem in . . .   **a.** Toronto

___ ② Police officers are on strike in . . .   **b.** Boston

___ ③ It's snowing very hard in . . .   **c.** Miami

___ ④ There aren't any problems in . . .   **d.** Sacramento

___ ⑤ Children aren't going to school in . . .   **e.** Chicago

BUILD YOUR VOCABULARY!
How Do You Get to Work?

I _____ .

- walk
- drive
- take the bus
- take the train
- take the subway
- take a taxi
- ride a bicycle
- ride a motor scooter
- ride a motorcycle

Getting Places

People around the world go to work or school in many different ways.

Some people take the subway.

Some people ride a bicycle.

Some people ride a motor scooter.

Some people even rollerblade!

How do people go to work or school in different countries you know?

FACT FILE

World's Largest Subway Systems

City	Number of Riders in a Year (in millions)	City	Number of Riders in a Year (in millions)
Moscow	3,160	Paris	1,120
Tokyo	2,740	Osaka	1,000
Mexico City	1,420	Hong Kong	779
Seoul	1,390	London	770
New York	1,130	Sao Paulo	701

Global Exchange

JeffZ: I live in a small apartment in the center of our city. I have a brother and two sisters. My brother's name is Kevin, and my sisters' names are Emily and Melissa. Our family has a dog and a bird. Our dog's name is Buster, and our bird's name is Lulu. I'm tall, and I have brown eyes. My hair is short and curly. It's usually black, but this week it's red. How about you? Where do you live? Do you have brothers or sisters? What are their names? Do you have a dog or a cat or another pet? What do you look like?

Send a message to a keypal. Tell about yourself.

What Are They Saying?

13

Can
Have to

- **Expressing Ability**
- **Occupations**
- **Looking for a Job**
- **Expressing Obligation**
- **Invitations**

VOCABULARY PREVIEW

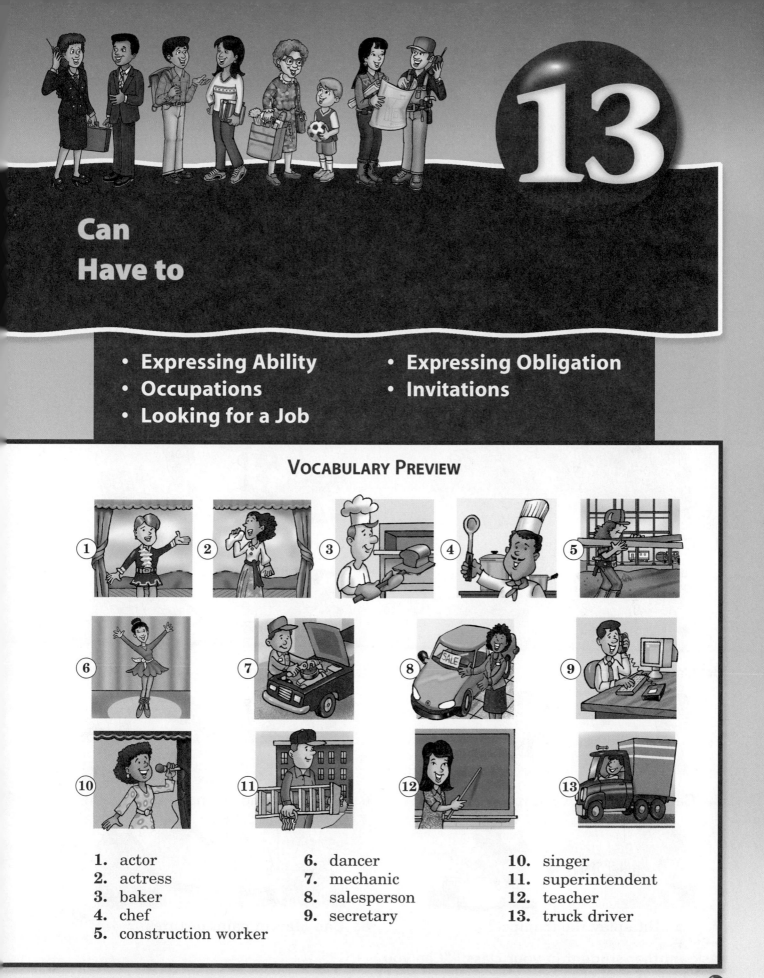

1. actor
2. actress
3. baker
4. chef
5. construction worker
6. dancer
7. mechanic
8. salesperson
9. secretary
10. singer
11. superintendent
12. teacher
13. truck driver

Can You?

I
He
She
It
We
You
They
} can / can't sing.
(cannot)

Can you sing?
Yes, I can.
No, I can't.

Can you speak Hungarian?

No, I can't. But I can speak Romanian.

1. Can Betty drive a bus?

2. Can Fred cook Italian food?

3. Can they ski?

4. Can you skate?

5. Can Roger use a cash register?

6. Can Judy and Donna play baseball?

7. Can Rita play the trumpet?

8. Can Marvin paint pictures?

Ask another student in your class: "Can you _____?"

Of Course They Can

A. Can Jack fix cars?

B. Of course he can.
He fixes cars every day. He's a mechanic.

1. Can Michael type?
secretary

2. Can Barbara teach?
teacher

3. Can Oscar bake pies and cakes?
baker

4. Can Jane drive a truck?
truck driver

5. Can Stanley cook?
chef

6. Can Claudia sing?
singer

7. Can Bruce and Helen dance?
dancers

8. Can Arthur act?
actor

9. Can Elizabeth and Katherine act?
actresses

THE ACE EMPLOYMENT SERVICE

Many people are sitting in the reception room at the Ace Employment Service. They're all looking for work, and they're hoping they can find jobs today.

Natalie is looking for a job as a secretary. She can type, she can file, and she can use business software on the computer. William is looking for a job as a building superintendent. He can paint walls, he can repair locks, and he can fix stoves and refrigerators.

Sandra is looking for a job as a construction worker. She can use tools, she can operate equipment, and she can build things. Nick is looking for a job as a salesperson. He can talk to customers, he can use a cash register, and he can take inventory. Stephanie and Tiffany are looking for jobs as actresses. They can sing, they can dance, and they can act.

Good luck, everybody! We hope you find the jobs you're looking for!

✔ READING *CHECK-UP*

Q & A

Natalie, William, Sandra, Nick, Stephanie, and Tiffany are having their interviews at the Ace Employment Service. Using this model, create dialogs based on the story.

A. What's your name?
B. *Natalie Kramer.*
A. Nice to meet you. Tell me, *Natalie*, what kind of job are you looking for?
B. I'm looking for a job as *a secretary*.
A. Tell me about your skills. What can you do?
B. I can *type*, I can *file*, and I can *use business software on the computer.*

LISTENING

CAN OR CAN'T?

Listen and choose the word you hear.

1. a. can   b. can't
2. a. can   b. can't
3. a. can   b. can't
4. a. can   b. can't
5. a. can   b. can't
6. a. can   b. can't

WHAT CAN THEY DO?

Listen and choose what each person can do.

1. a. file   b. type
2. a. cook   b. bake
3. a. repair locks   b. repair stoves
4. a. drive a truck   b. drive a bus
5. a. teach French   b. teach English
6. a. take inventory b. paint

ON YOUR OWN   *Your Skills*

Think about your skills. What can you do? What CAN'T you do? Make two lists. Then talk about your lists with other students.

Things I Can Do	Things I Can't Do

They Can't Go to Herbert's Party

I			
We	} have to		
You			
They			work.
He			
She	} has to		
It			

Herbert is depressed. He's having a party today, but his friends can't go to his party. They're all busy.

A. Can you go to Herbert's party?

B. No, I can't. I have to work.

A. Can Michael go to Herbert's party?

B. No, he can't. He has to go to the doctor.

1. *you and Tom?*
fix our car

2. *Susan?*
go to the dentist

3. *your children?*
do their homework

4. *John?*
wash his clothes

5. *your parents?*
clean their apartment

6. Can YOU go to Herbert's party?

Apologizing

A. Can you go *to a movie* with me on *Saturday?*
B. I'm sorry. I can't. I have to *clean my apartment.*

Practice the interactions on this page, using "I'm sorry" to apologize.

INTERACTIONS

A. Can you _____ with me on _____?
B. I'm sorry. I can't. I have to _____.

Practice conversations with other students. Practice inviting, apologizing, and giving reasons.

go to a soccer game

have lunch

have dinner

go swimming

go shopping

go dancing

go skating

go skiing

go bowling

APPLYING FOR A DRIVER'S LICENSE

Henry is annoyed. He's applying for a driver's license, and he's upset about all the things he has to do.

First, he has to go to the Motor Vehicles Department and pick up an application form. He can't ask for the form on the telephone, and he can't ask for it by mail. He has to go downtown and pick up the form in person.

He has to fill out the form in duplicate. He can't use a pencil. He has to use a pen. He can't use blue ink. He has to use black ink. And he can't write in script. He has to print.

He also has to attach two photographs to the application. They can't be old photographs. They have to be new. They can't be large. They have to be small. And they can't be black and white. They have to be color.

Then he has to submit his application. He has to wait in a long line to pay his application fee. He has to wait in another long line to have an eye examination. And believe it or not, he has to wait in ANOTHER long line to take a written test!

Finally, he has to take a road test. He has to start the car. He has to make a right turn, a left turn, and a U-turn. And he even has to park his car on a crowded city street.

No wonder Henry is annoyed! He's applying for his driver's license, and he can't believe all the things he has to do.

✔ READING *CHECK-UP*

WHAT'S THE ANSWER?

1. Can Henry apply for a driver's license on the telephone?
2. Where does he have to go to apply for a license?
3. How does he have to fill out the form?
4. How many photographs does he have to attach to the application?
5. What kind of photographs do they have to be?
6. What does Henry have to do during the road test?

FIX THIS SIGN!

This sign at the Motor Vehicles Department is wrong. The things people have to do are in the wrong order. On a separate sheet of paper, fix the sign based on the story.

How to Apply for a Driver's License

Have an eye examination.
Pay the application fee.
Take a road test.
Pick up an application form.
Take a written test.
Fill out the form in duplicate.

IN YOUR OWN WORDS

FOR WRITING AND DISCUSSION

Explain how to apply for one of the following: a passport, a marriage license, a loan, or something else. In your explanation, use "You have to."*

* "You have to" = "A person has to"

PRONUNCIATION *Can & Can't*

Listen. Then say it.

I can type.

She can teach.

Yes, I can.

No, he can't.

Say it. Then listen.

We can dance.

He can sing.

Yes, they can.

No, she can't.

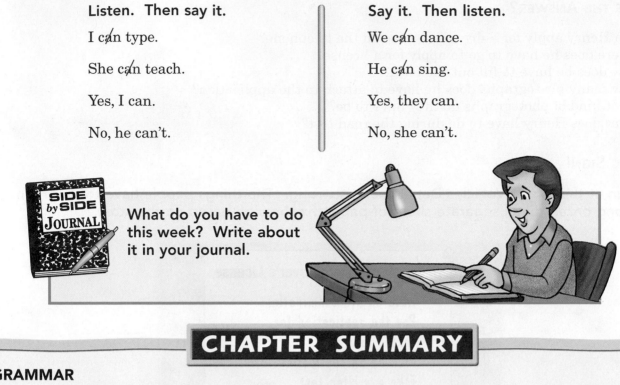

SIDE *by* SIDE JOURNAL

What do you have to do this week? Write about it in your journal.

CHAPTER SUMMARY

GRAMMAR

CAN

Can	I he she it we you they	sing?

I He She It We You They	can / can't	sing.

Yes,	I he she it we you they	can.

No,	I he she it we you they	can't.

HAVE TO

I We You They	have to	work.
He She It	has to	

KEY VOCABULARY

OCCUPATIONS

actor
actress
baker
chef
construction
  worker

dancer
mechanic
salesperson
secretary
singer
superintendent

teacher
truck driver

SKILLS

act
bake
build
cook
dance
drive

file
fix
operate
paint
repair
sing

speak *Spanish*
take inventory
talk
teach
type
use

Future: Going to
Time Expressions
Want to

- **Describing Future Plans and Intentions**
- **Expressing Wants**
- **Weather Forecasts**
- **Telling Time**
- **Making Predictions**

VOCABULARY PREVIEW

Time

2:00
It's two o'clock.

2:15
It's two fifteen.
It's a quarter after two.

2:30
It's two thirty.
It's half past two.

2:45
It's two forty-five.
It's a quarter to three.

Months of the Year

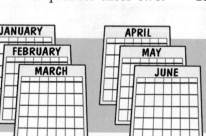

JANUARY	APRIL	JULY	OCTOBER
FEBRUARY	MAY	AUGUST	NOVEMBER
MARCH	JUNE	SEPTEMBER	DECEMBER

Seasons

spring   summer   fall/autumn   winter

What Are They Going to Do Tomorrow?

What am I is { he she it } are { we you they } **going to do?**	(I am) I'm (He is) He's (She is) She's (It is) It's (We are) We're (You are) You're (They are) They're **going to read.**

A. What's Fred going to do tomorrow?

B. He's going to fix his car.

1. *Jenny?*

2. *Cathy and Dave?*

3. *Tony?*

4. *you and your brother?*

5. *Andrew?*

6. *Ashley?*

They're Going to the Beach

They're going (to go) to the beach.	=	They're going to the beach.
		They're going to go to the beach.
We're going (to go) swimming.	=	We're going swimming.
		We're going to go swimming.

today	tomorrow
this morning	tomorrow morning
this afternoon	tomorrow afternoon
this evening	tomorrow evening
tonight	tomorrow night

A. What are Mr. and Mrs. Brown going to do tomorrow?

B. They're going (to go) to the beach.

1. What's Anita going to do this morning?

2. What are Steve and Brenda going to do tonight?

3. What's Fernando going to do tomorrow evening?

4. What are you and your friends going to do tomorrow afternoon?

What are YOU going to do tomorrow?

129

When Are You Going to . . .?

Time Expressions

this _____
next _____
{ week / month / year
Sunday / Monday / Tuesday / Wednesday / Thursday /
Friday / Saturday
January / February / March / April / May / June /
July / August / September / October /
November / December
spring / summer / fall (autumn) / winter }

right now
right away
immediately
at once

Practice conversations with other students. Use any of the time expressions on page 130.

1. When are you going to clean your garage?

2. When are you going to call your grandmother?

3. When are you going to fix your bicycle?

4. When are you going to visit us?

5. When are you going to wash your car?

6. When are you going to plant flowers this year?

7. When are you going to write to your Aunt Martha?

8. Mr. Smith! When are you going to iron those pants?

Now ask another student: "When are you going to _____?"

READING

HAPPY NEW YEAR!

It's December thirty-first, New Year's Eve. Ruth and Larry Carter are celebrating the holiday with their children, Nicole and Jonathan. The Carters are a very happy family this New Year's Eve. Next year is going to be a very good year for the entire family.

Next year, Ruth and Larry are going to take a long vacation. They're going to visit Larry's brother in Alaska. Nicole is going to finish high school. She's going to move to San Francisco and begin college. Jonathan is going to get his driver's license. He's going to save a lot of money and buy a used car.

As you can see, the Carters are really looking forward to next year. It's going to be a very happy year for all of them.

Happy New Year!

✔ READING CHECK-UP

COMPUTER CHAT

Fill in the missing words. Then practice this computer chat with another student.

AlexR: Jonathan, _____¹ do next year?

JonC: _____² get my driver's license.

AlexR: And your sister? _____³ do next year?

JonC: _____⁴ begin college.

AlexR: How about your parents? _____⁵ next year?

JonC: _____⁶ take a long vacation.

AlexR: Well, Happy New Year, Jonathan!

JonC: Happy New Year!

LISTENING

Listen and choose the words you hear.

1. a. Tomorrow.   b. This March.
2. a. Next December.   b. Next November.
3. a. Next month.   b. Next Monday.
4. a. This evening.   b. This morning.
5. a. This summer.   b. This Sunday.

6. a. This Tuesday.   b. This Thursday.
7. a. This afternoon.   b. Tomorrow afternoon.
8. a. Next year.   b. Next week.
9. a. Next winter.   b. Next summer.
10. a. This month.   b. At once.

What's the Forecast?

I We You They	want to
He She It	wants to study.

A. What are you going to do tomorrow?

B. I don't know. I want to **go swimming**, but I think the weather is going to be bad.

A. Really? What's the forecast?

B. The radio says it's going to **rain**.

A. That's strange! According to the newspaper, it's going to **be sunny**.

B. I hope you're right. I REALLY want to **go swimming**.

1. *have a picnic*
   rain
   be nice

2. *go to the beach*
   be cloudy
   be sunny

3. *go sailing*
   be foggy
   be clear

4. *go skiing*
   be warm
   snow

5. *work in my garden*
   be very hot
   be cool

6. *take my children to the zoo*
   be cold
   be warm

Discuss in class: What's the weather today?
What's the weather forecast for tomorrow?

What Time Is It?

2:00
It's two o'clock.

2:15
It's two fifteen.
It's a quarter after two.

2:30
It's two thirty.
It's half past two.

2:45
It's two forty-five.
It's a quarter to three.

It's noon.
It's twelve noon.

It's midnight.
It's twelve midnight.

A. What time does the movie begin?

B. It begins at 8:00.

A. At 8:00?! Oh no! We're going to be late!

B. Why? What time is it?

A. It's 7:30! We have to leave RIGHT NOW!

B. I can't leave now. I'm SHAVING!

A. Please try to hurry! I don't want to be late for the movie.

A. What time does _____?

B. It _____ at _____.

A. At _____?! Oh no! We're going to be late!

B. Why? What time is it?

A. It's _____! We have to leave RIGHT NOW!

B. I can't leave now. I'm _____!

A. Please try to hurry! I don't want to be late for the _____.

1. What time does the football game begin?
3:00 / 2:30
taking a bath

2. What time does the bus leave?
7:15 / 6:45
packing my suitcase

3. What time does the train leave?
5:30 / 5:15
taking a shower

4. What time does the concert begin?
8:00 / 7:45
looking for my pants

How to Say It!

Asking the Time

A. { What time is it?
{ What's the time?

B. It's 4:00.

A. { Can you tell me the time?
{ Do you know the time?

B. Yes. It's 4:00.

Practice conversations with other students. Ask the time in different ways.

THE FORTUNE TELLER

Walter is visiting Madame Sophia, the famous fortune teller. He's wondering about his future, and Madame Sophia is telling him what is going to happen next year. According to Madame Sophia, next year is going to be a very interesting year in Walter's life.

In January he's going to meet a very nice woman and fall in love.

In February he's going to get married.

In March he's going to take a trip to a warm, sunny place.

In April he's going to have a bad cold.

In May his parents are going to move to a beautiful city in California.

In June there's going to be a fire in his apartment building, and he's going to have to find a new place to live.

In July his friends are going to give him a DVD player for his birthday.

In August his boss is going to fire him.

In September he's going to start a new job with a very big salary.

In October he's going to be in a car accident, but he isn't going to be hurt.

In November he's going to be on a television game show and win a million dollars.

And in December he's going to become a father!

According to Madame Sophia, a lot is going to happen in Walter's life next year. But Walter isn't sure he believes any of this. He doesn't believe in fortunes or fortune tellers. But in January he's going to get a haircut and buy a lot of new clothes, just in case Madame Sophia is right and he meets a wonderful woman and falls in love!

✔ READING *CHECK-UP*

Q & A

Walter is talking to Madame Sophia. Using these models, create dialogs based on the story.

A. Tell me, what's going to happen in *January*?
B. In *January*? Oh! *January* is going to be a very good month!
A. Really? What's going to happen?
B. *You're going to meet a very nice woman and fall in love.*
A. Oh! That's wonderful!

A. Tell me, what's going to happen in *April*?
B. In *April*? Oh! *April* is going to be a very bad month!
A. Really? What's going to happen?
B. *You're going to have a bad cold.*
A. Oh! That's terrible!

PRONUNCIATION *Going to & Want to*

going to = gonna
want to = wanna

Listen. Then say it.

I'm going to study.

It's going to rain.

We want to go swimming.

They want to leave.

Say it. Then listen.

He's going to cook.

They're going to paint.

I want to read.

We want to go to the beach.

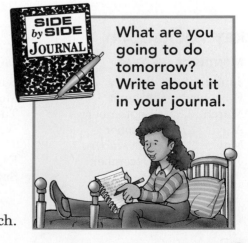

What are you going to do tomorrow? Write about it in your journal.

GRAMMAR

FUTURE: GOING TO

What	am	I	going to do?
	is	he she it	
	are	we you they	

(I am)	I'm	going to read.
(He is)	He's	
(She is)	She's	
(It is)	It's	
(We are)	We're	
(You are)	You're	
(They are)	They're	

TIME EXPRESSIONS

I'm going to wash my clothes	today.	tomorrow.	right now.
	this morning.	tomorrow morning.	right away.
	this afternoon.	tomorrow afternoon.	immediately.
	this evening.	tomorrow evening.	at once.
	tonight.	tomorrow night.	

I'm going to fix my car	this next	week / month / year.
		Sunday / Monday / Tuesday / . . . / Saturday.
		January / February / March / . . . / December.
		spring / summer / fall (autumn) / winter.

It's	eleven o'clock.		11:00
	eleven fifteen.	a quarter after eleven.	11:15
	eleven thirty.	half past eleven.	11:30
	eleven forty-five.	a quarter to twelve.	11:45

WANT TO

I We You They	want to	study.
He She It	wants to	

KEY VOCABULARY

MONTHS OF THE YEAR

January	July
February	August
March	September
April	October
May	November
June	December

DAYS OF THE WEEK

Sunday
Monday
Tuesday
Wednesday
Thursday
Friday
Saturday

SEASONS

spring
summer
fall/autumn
winter

Time Zones

What time is it right now? What time is it in other parts of the world? How do you know?

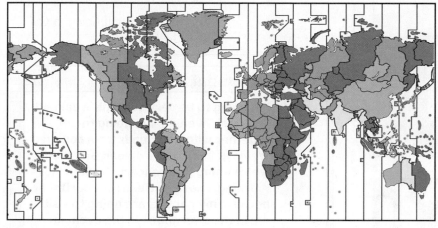

There are 24 time zones around the world. In each time zone, it is a different hour of the day. The time zone that is east of your time zone is one hour ahead. The time zone to your west is one hour behind. So, for example, when it's 10:00 in Chicago, it's 11:00 in New York, it's 9:00 in Denver, and it's 8:00 in Los Angeles.

New Zealand is 12 time zones to the east of London. Therefore, when it's midnight in London and people are sleeping, it's noon the next day in New Zealand and people are eating lunch!

FACT FILE

A Moment in the Life of the World

TIME AND DAY	PLACE
5:00 A.M.* Monday morning	Los Angeles, USA
7:00 A.M. Monday morning	Mexico City, Mexico
8:00 A.M. Monday morning	New York City, USA; Toronto, Canada
9:00 A.M. Monday morning	Caracas, Venezuela
10:00 A.M. Monday morning	Rio de Janeiro, Brazil; Buenos Aires, Argentina
1:00 P.M.* Monday afternoon	London, England; Lisbon, Portugal
2:00 P.M. Monday afternoon	Paris, France; Madrid, Spain; Rome, Italy
3:00 P.M. Monday afternoon	Athens, Greece; Istanbul, Turkey
4:00 P.M. Monday afternoon	Moscow, Russia
9:00 P.M. Monday night	Hong Kong, China
10:00 P.M. Monday night	Seoul, Korea; Tokyo, Japan
12:00 A.M. Tuesday morning	Sydney, Australia

*A.M. = 12:00 midnight to 11:59 in the morning   P.M. = 12:00 noon to 11:59 at night

BUILD YOUR VOCABULARY!

Occupations

A. What do you do?
B. I'm a / an _____ .

■ architect

■ carpenter

■ cashier

■ farmer

■ lawyer

■ painter

■ pilot

■ translator

■ waiter

■ waitress

AROUND THE WORLD

Time and Culture

People in different cultures think of time in different ways.

In your culture, do people arrive on time for work? Do people arrive on time for appointments? Do people arrive on time for parties? Tell about time in your culture.

Thank You for Calling the Multiplex Cinema!

_c_ **1**

____ **2**

____ **3**

____ **4**

____ **5**

a. *The Fortune Teller*

b. *Tomorrow Is Right Now*

c. *The Spanish Dancer*

d. *The Time Zone Machine*

e. *When Are You Going to Call the Plumber?*

Global Exchange

JulieP: I'm going to be very busy this weekend. On Friday evening, I'm going to get together with my friends from college. We're going to have dinner, and then we're going to a concert. On Saturday morning, I have to clean my apartment because my parents are going to visit me in the afternoon. In the evening, we're going to go bowling. On Sunday I'm going to teach my Sunday school class in the morning, I'm going to a soccer game in the afternoon, and I'm going to wash my clothes in the evening. How about you? What are you going to do this weekend?

Send a message to a keypal. Tell about your plans for the weekend.

What Are They Saying?

Past Tense:
Regular Verbs
Introduction to Irregular Verbs

- **Past Actions and Activities**
- **Ailments**
- **Describing an Event**
- **Making a Doctor's Appointment**

VOCABULARY PREVIEW

1. headache
2. stomachache
3. toothache

4. backache
5. earache
6. cold

7. fever
8. cough
9. sore throat

How Do You Feel Today?

A. How do you feel today?

B. Not so good.

A. What's the matter?

B. I have a headache.

A. I'm sorry to hear that.

1. *stomachache*

2. *toothache*

3. *backache*

4. *earache*

5. *cold*

6. *fever*

7. *cough*

8. *sore throat*

How to Say It!

Saying How You Feel

How do you feel today?

I feel great! I feel fine. I feel okay.

I'm glad to hear that.

How do you feel today?

So-so. Not so good. I feel terrible.

I'm sorry to hear that.

Practice conversations with other students.

142

What Did You Do Yesterday?

t
I work every day.
I work**ed** yesterday.

d
I play the piano every day.
I play**ed** the piano yesterday.

id
I rest every day.
I rest**ed** yesterday.

What did you do yesterday?

I worked.

t

1. *cook*

2. *wash my car*

3. *fix my bicycle*

4. *brush my teeth*

5. *watch TV*

6. *type**

7. *dance**

8. *bake**

d

9. *clean*

10. *play the piano*

11. *yawn*

12. *listen to music*

13. *shave**

14. *smile**

15. *cry†*

16. *study†*

id

17. *shout*

18. *rest*

19. *plant flowers*

20. *wait for the bus*

* type – typed   shave – shaved   † cry – cried
  dance – danced   smile – smiled   study – studied
  bake – baked

143

What's the Matter?

I / We / You / They	work every day.
He / She / It	works every day.

I / We / You / They	worked yesterday.
He / She / It	

A. How does David feel?

B. Not so good.

A. What's the matter?

B. He has a backache.

A. A backache? How did he get it?

B. He played basketball all day.*

* Or: all morning / all afternoon / all evening / all night

---

1. *Brian*

2. *Linda*

3. *you*

4. *Gary*

5. *Maria*

6. *Charlie*

7. *Mrs. Clark*

8. *you*

9. *Carlos*

 144

| eat – ate | sing – sang | drink – drank | sit – sat | ride – rode |

10. *Daniel*

11. *Jennifer*

12. *you*

13. *Sarah*

14. *you*

15. *Tim*

ROLE PLAY *Do You Want to Make an Appointment?*

You don't feel very well today. Call the doctor's office and make an appointment.

A. Doctor's Office.

B. Hello. This is _____.

A. Hello, Mr./Ms./Mrs. _____.
How are you?

B. Not so good.

A. I'm sorry to hear that. What seems to be
the problem?

B. I _____ all _____ yesterday,
and now I have a TERRIBLE _____.

A. I see. Do you want to make an
appointment?

B. Yes, please.

A. Can you come in tomorrow at
_____ o'clock?

B. At _____ o'clock? Yes. That's fine.
Thank you.

THE WILSONS' PARTY

Mr. and Mrs. Wilson invited all their friends and neighbors to a party last night. They stayed home all day yesterday and prepared for the party.

In the morning the Wilsons worked outside. Their daughter, Margaret, cleaned the yard. Their son, Bob, painted the fence. Mrs. Wilson planted flowers in the garden, and Mr. Wilson fixed their broken front steps.

In the afternoon the Wilsons worked inside the house. Margaret washed the floors and vacuumed the living room carpet. Bob dusted the furniture and cleaned the basement. Mr. and Mrs. Wilson stayed in the kitchen all afternoon. He cooked spaghetti for dinner, and she baked apple pies for dessert.

The Wilsons finished all their work at six o'clock. Their house looked beautiful inside and out!

The Wilsons' guests arrived at about 7:30. After they arrived, they all sat in the living room. They ate cheese and crackers, drank lemonade, and talked. Some people talked about their children. Other people talked about the weather. And EVERYBODY talked about how beautiful the Wilsons' house looked inside and out!

The Wilsons served dinner in the dining room at 9:00. Everybody enjoyed the meal very much. They liked Mr. Wilson's spaghetti and they "loved" Mrs. Wilson's apple pie. In fact, everybody asked for seconds.

After dinner everybody sat in the living room again. First, Bob Wilson played the piano and his sister, Margaret, sang. Then, Mr. and Mrs. Wilson showed a video of their trip to Hawaii. After that, they turned on the music and everybody danced.

As you can see, the Wilsons' guests enjoyed the party very much. In fact, nobody wanted to go home!

✔ READING *CHECK-UP*

WHAT'S THE ANSWER?

1. What did Margaret and Bob Wilson do in the morning?
2. How did Mr. and Mrs. Wilson prepare for the party in the afternoon?
3. When did the guests arrive?
4. Where did the guests sit after they arrived?
5. What did they eat and drink before dinner?
6. What did Margaret do after dinner?
7. What did Mr. and Mrs. Wilson do after dinner?

LISTENING

Listen and choose the word you hear.

1. a. plant   b. planted
2. a. work   b. worked
3. a. study   b. studied
4. a. sit   b. sat
5. a. drink   b. drank
6. a. wait   b. waited

7. a. finish   b. finished
8. a. invite   b. invited
9. a. eat   b. ate
10. a. clean   b. cleaned
11. a. wash   b. washed
12. a. watch   b. watched

IN YOUR OWN WORDS

FOR WRITING OR DISCUSSION

A PARTY

Tell about a party you enjoyed.

What did you eat?
What did you drink?
What did people do at the party?
   (eat, dance, talk about . . .)

147

PRONUNCIATION *Past Tense Endings*

Put these words in the correct column. Then practice saying the words in each column.

| cleaned | danced | dusted | painted | played | studied | talked | typed | waited |

t	**d**	**ɪd**
	cleaned	

Listen. Then say it.

I cooked, I cleaned, and I dusted.

I worked, I played, and I planted flowers.

Say it. Then listen.

I typed, I studied, and I painted.

I talked, I cried, and I shouted.

SIDE *by* SIDE JOURNAL

What did you eat yesterday? What did you drink? Write about it in your journal.

CHAPTER SUMMARY

GRAMMAR

PAST TENSE

I He She It We You They	worked yesterday.

[t]	I worked. I danced.
[d]	I cleaned. I played.
[ɪd]	I rested. I shouted.

IRREGULAR VERBS

eat – ate
drink – drank
ride – rode
sing – sang
sit – sat

KEY VOCABULARY

AILMENTS

backache	headache
cold	sore throat
cough	stomachache
earache	toothache
fever	

TALKING ABOUT HOW YOU FEEL

How are you?
How do you feel today?

What's the matter?

I feel great!
I feel fine.
I feel okay.

So-so.
Not so good.
I feel terrible.

Past Tense:

Yes/No Questions
Short Answers
Time Expressions

WH-Questions
More Irregular Verbs

- **Reporting Past Actions and Activities**
- **Giving Reasons**
- **Giving Excuses**

VOCABULARY PREVIEW

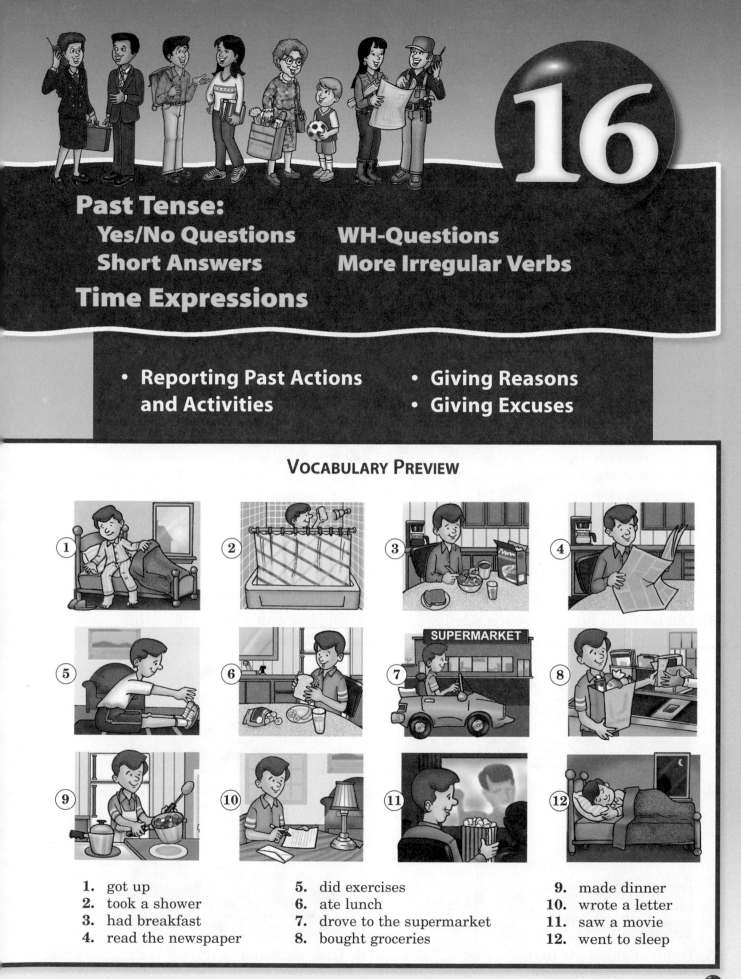

1. got up
2. took a shower
3. had breakfast
4. read the newspaper
5. did exercises
6. ate lunch
7. drove to the supermarket
8. bought groceries
9. made dinner
10. wrote a letter
11. saw a movie
12. went to sleep

I Brushed My Teeth

I worked.
I didn't work.
(did not)

Did you work?
Yes, I did.
No, I didn't.

today	*yesterday*
this morning	yesterday morning
this afternoon	yesterday afternoon
this evening	yesterday evening
tonight	last night

Did you brush your hair this morning?

No, I didn't. I brushed my teeth.

1. Did he wash his windows yesterday morning?

2. Did she paint her kitchen this afternoon?

3. Did they study English last night?

4. Did you and your friends play tennis yesterday afternoon?

5. Did he bake a pie today?

6. Did you listen to the news this morning?

We Went to the Supermarket

I went.
I didn't go.
(did not)

Did you go?
Yes, I did.
No, I didn't.

go
went

take
took

1. Did you take the subway this morning?

have
had

2. Did he have a headache last night?

get
got

3. Did Wanda get up at 9:00 this morning?

make
made

4. Did your children make dinner today?

buy
bought

5. Did Michael buy a car yesterday?

do
did

6. Did they do their homework last night?

write
wrote

7. Did Tommy write to his girlfriend this week?

read
read

8. Did you read the newspaper this afternoon?

TALK ABOUT IT! *What Did They Do Yesterday?*

| Yes, { I / he / she / it / we / you / they } did. | No, { I / he / she / it / we / you / they } didn't. |

Betty fixed her car yesterday morning.
She washed her windows yesterday afternoon.
She listened to music last night.

Bob read the newspaper yesterday morning.
He went to the library yesterday afternoon.
He wrote letters last night.

Nick and Nancy went to the supermarket
   yesterday morning.
They bought a new car yesterday afternoon.
They cleaned their apartment last night.

Jennifer did her exercises yesterday
   morning.
She planted flowers yesterday afternoon.
She took a bath last night.

**Using these models, talk about the people
above with other students in your class.**

A. Did *Betty fix her car yesterday morning?*

B. Yes, *she* did.

A. Did *Bob go to the library last night?*

B. No, *he* didn't. *He went to the library
   yesterday afternoon.*

How About You?

What did you do yesterday
   morning?
What did you do yesterday
   afternoon?
What did you do last night?

How to Say It!

Giving an Excuse

A. I'm sorry I'm late. *I missed the bus.*

B. I see.

Practice the interactions on this page.
Apologize and give excuses.

INTERACTIONS

A. I'm sorry I'm late. _____.

B. I see.

I missed the _____.
(bus / train . . .)

I had a _____ this morning.
(headache / stomachache / . . .)

I had to go to the _____.
(doctor / dentist / . . .)

I forgot* my _____ and had to
go back home and get it.
(briefcase / backpack / . . .)

A thief stole* my _____.
(bicycle / car / . . .)

THINK ABOUT IT! *Good Excuses & Bad Excuses*

The people above have good excuses. Here are some BAD excuses:

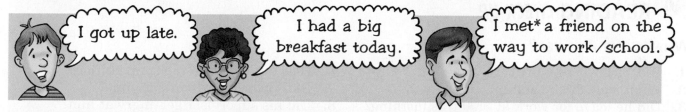

I got up late.

I had a big breakfast today.

I met* a friend on the way to work / school.

Discuss with other students: What are some good excuses? What are some bad
excuses? Why are these excuses good or bad?

* forget – forgot   steal – stole   meet – met

LATE FOR WORK

Victor usually gets up at 7 A.M. He does his morning exercises for twenty minutes, he takes a long shower, he has a big breakfast, and he leaves for work at 8:00. He usually drives his car to work and gets there at 8:30.

This morning, however, he didn't get up at 7 A.M. He got up at 6:30. He didn't do his morning exercises for twenty minutes. He did them for only five minutes. He didn't take a long shower. He took a very quick shower. He didn't have a big breakfast. He had a very small breakfast. He didn't leave for work at 8:00. He left for work at 7:00.

Victor didn't drive his car to work this morning. He drove it to the repair shop. Then he walked a mile to the train station, and he waited for the train for fifteen minutes. After he got off the train, he walked half a mile to his office.

Even though Victor got up early and rushed out of the house this morning, he didn't get to work on time. He got there forty-five minutes late. When his supervisor saw him, she got angry and she shouted at him for five minutes. Poor Victor! He really tried to get to work on time this morning.

✔ READING *CHECK-UP*

WHAT'S THE ANSWER?

1. Did Victor get up at 7 A.M. today?
2. What time did he get up?
3. Did he leave for work at 8:00 this morning?
4. What time did he leave for work?
5. Did he drive his car to the repair shop today?

6. How did he get to the train station?
7. Did Victor get to work on time?
8. Did his supervisor get angry at him?
9. What did she do?

Which is Correct?

1. Victor (got up   didn't get up) at 6:30 A.M. this morning.
2. He (did   didn't do) his exercises for twenty minutes today.
3. He (took   didn't take) a very quick shower this morning.
4. He (left   didn't leave) for work at 8:00 this morning.
5. He (took   didn't take) the train to work today.
6. He (got   didn't get) to work on time this morning.

LISTENING

Listen and put a check next to all the things these people did today.

Carla's Day
___ got up early
___ got up late
___ took a bath
___ took a shower
___ had breakfast
___ had lunch
___ took the subway
___ took the bus
___ met her brother
___ met her mother
___ had dinner
___ made dinner
___ saw a movie
___ saw a play

Brian's Day
___ fixed his car
___ fixed his bicycle
___ cleaned his garage
___ cleaned his yard
___ painted his bedroom
___ planted flowers
___ washed his windows
___ watched TV
___ read the newspaper
___ read a magazine
___ rode his bicycle
___ wrote to his brother
___ took a shower
___ took a bath

COMPLETE THE STORY

Complete the story with the correct forms of the verbs.

buy	eat	get	go	make	see	sit	take

SHIRLEY'S DAY OFF

Shirley enjoyed her day off yesterday. She
_____¹ up late, _____² jogging in the park,
_____³ a long shower, and _____⁴ a big breakfast.
In the afternoon, she _____⁵ a movie with her sister.
Then she _____⁶ groceries at the supermarket, and
she _____⁷ a big dinner for her parents. After dinner,
Shirley and her parents _____⁸ in the living room and
talked. Shirley had a very nice day off yesterday.

How About You?

Tell about a day off YOU enjoyed. What did you do in the morning? in the afternoon? in the evening?

Listen. Then say it.

Did you go to the bank?

Did you brush your hair?

Did you listen to the news?

Did you take the subway?

Say it. Then listen.

Did you go to the supermarket?

Did you play tennis?

Did you read the newspaper?

Did you see a movie?

What did you do yesterday? Write in your journal about all the things you did.

CHAPTER SUMMARY

GRAMMAR

PAST TENSE:
YES/NO QUESTIONS

Did	I he she it we you they	work?

SHORT ANSWERS

Yes,	I he she it we you they	did.

No,	I he she it we you they	didn't.

PAST TENSE:
WH-QUESTIONS

What did	I he she it we you they	do?

TIME EXPRESSIONS

Did you study English	yesterday? yesterday morning? yesterday afternoon? yesterday evening? last night?

KEY VOCABULARY

IRREGULAR VERBS

buy – bought	eat – ate	go – went	meet – met	steal – stole
do – did	forget – forgot	have – had	read – read	take – took
drive – drove	get – got	make – made	see – saw	write – wrote

To Be: Past Tense

- Television Commercials
- Describing Physical States and Emotions
- Telling About the Past
- Biographies and Autobiographies

VOCABULARY PREVIEW

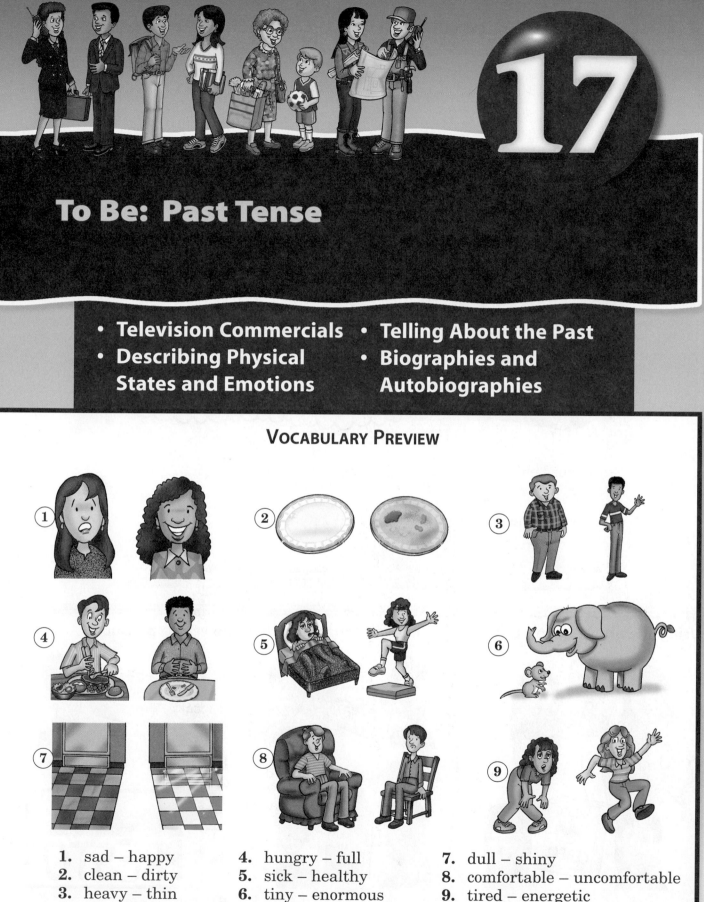

1. sad – happy
2. clean – dirty
3. heavy – thin
4. hungry – full
5. sick – healthy
6. tiny – enormous
7. dull – shiny
8. comfortable – uncomfortable
9. tired – energetic

PRESTO Commercials

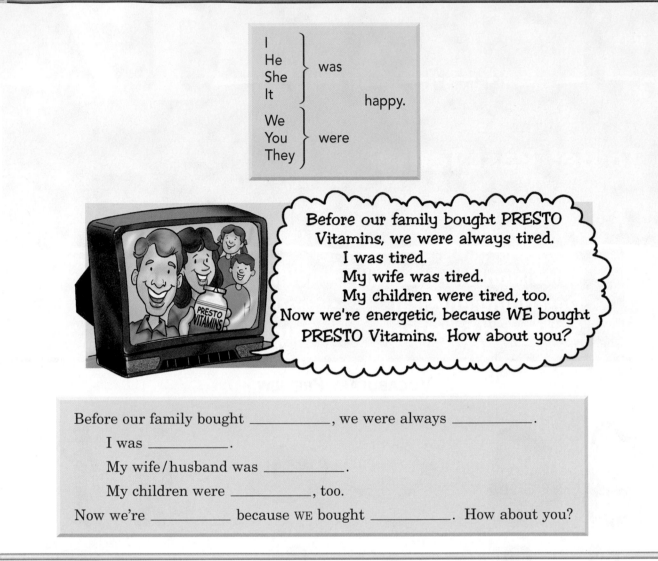

I
He
She
It   } was
                    happy.
We
You   } were
They

Before our family bought PRESTO Vitamins, we were always tired.
I was tired.
My wife was tired.
My children were tired, too.
Now we're energetic, because WE bought PRESTO Vitamins. How about you?

Before our family bought _____, we were always _____.
   I was _____.
   My wife/husband was _____.
   My children were _____, too.
Now we're _____ because WE bought _____. How about you?

Using the above script, prepare commercials for these other fine PRESTO products.

1. sad   happy   2. hungry   full   3. dirty   clean

4. sick   healthy   5. heavy   thin   6. _____ _____

Before I Bought PRESTO Shampoo

Before I bought PRESTO Shampoo, my hair **was** always dirty. Now **it's** clean!

1. Before we bought PRESTO Toothpaste, our teeth _____ yellow. Now _____ white!

2. Before we bought PRESTO Paint, our house _____ ugly. Now _____ beautiful!

3. Before I bought a PRESTO armchair, I _____ uncomfortable. Now _____ very comfortable!

4. Before we bought PRESTO Dog Food, our dog _____ tiny. Now _____ enormous!

5. Before I bought PRESTO Window Cleaner, my windows _____ dirty. Now _____ clean!

6. Before we bought PRESTO Floor Wax, our kitchen floor _____ dull. Now _____ shiny!

How to Say It!

Recommending Products

A. Can you recommend a good *toothpaste*?
B. Yes. I recommend *PRESTO Toothpaste*. It's very good.
A. Thanks for the recommendation.

Practice conversations with other students. Make recommendations about real products.

Were You at the Ballgame Last Night?

I He She It	wasn't (was not)
We You They	weren't (were not)

A. Were you at the ballgame last night?

B. No, I wasn't. I was at the movies.

1. Was Albert happy yesterday?

2. Were they at home this morning?

3. Was it cold yesterday?

4. Was your grandfather a doctor?

5. Was I a quiet baby?

6. Were you at home last weekend?

7. Was Gloria on time for her plane?

8. Were your children late for the school bus?

9. Was the food good at the restaurant?

Did You Sleep Well Last Night?

| I / He / She / We / You / They | did / didn't | I / He / She | was / wasn't |
| | | We / You / They | were / weren't |

A. Did you sleep well last night?
B. Yes, I did. I was tired.

A. Did Roger sleep well last night?
B. No, he didn't. He wasn't tired.

1. Did Frank have a big breakfast today?
Yes, _____. _____ hungry.

2. Did Thelma have a big breakfast today?
No, _____. _____ hungry.

3. Did Mr. Chen go to the doctor yesterday?
Yes, _____. _____ sick.

4. Did Mrs. Chen go to the doctor yesterday?
No, _____. _____ sick.

5. Did Billy finish his milk?
Yes, _____. _____ thirsty.

6. Did Katie finish her milk?
No, _____. _____ thirsty.

7. Did Sonia miss the train?
Yes, _____. _____ late.

8. Did Stuart miss the train?
No , _____. _____ late.

161

READING

MARIA GOMEZ

Maria Gomez was born in Peru. She grew* up in a small village. She began* school when she was six years old. She went to elementary school, but she didn't go to high school. Her family was very poor, and she had to go to work when she was thirteen years old. She worked on an assembly line in a shoe factory.

When Maria was seventeen years old, her family moved to the United States. First they lived in Los Angeles, and then they moved to San Francisco. When Maria arrived in the United States, she wasn't very happy. She missed her friends back in Peru, and she didn't speak one word of English. She began to study English at night, and she worked in a factory during the day.

Maria studied very hard. She learned English, and she got a good job as a secretary. Maria still studies at night, but now she studies advertising at a business school. She wants to work for an advertising company some day and write commercials.

Maria still misses her friends back home, but she communicates with them very often over the Internet. She's very happy now, and she's looking forward to an exciting future.

✔ READING CHECK-UP

WHAT'S THE ANSWER?

1. Where was Maria born?
2. Did she grow up in a large city?
3. When did she begin school?
4. What happened when Maria was seventeen years old?
5. Why was Maria unhappy when she arrived in the United States?
6. What is Maria's occupation?
7. What does she want to do in the future?
8. How does Maria communicate with her friends back home?

* grow – grew   begin – began

WHAT'S THE ORDER?

Put these sentences in the correct order based on the story.

____ Maria's family moved to the United States.
____ Maria studies advertising now.
__1__ Maria grew up in a small village.
____ Maria's family moved to San Francisco.
____ Maria worked in a shoe factory.
____ Maria began to study English at night.
____ Maria went to elementary school.
____ Maria's family lived in Los Angeles.
____ Maria got a job as a secretary.

LISTENING

Listen and choose the correct answer.

1. a. They were sick.
   b. They're sick now.
2. a. Their old chairs were comfortable.
   b. Their new chairs are comfortable.
3. a. Lucy was very thirsty.
   b. Lucy wasn't thirsty.
4. a. Fred was on time this morning.
   b. Fred wasn't on time this morning.
5. a. Peter and Mary were at work yesterday.
   b. Peter and Mary are at work today.
6. a. Their kitchen floor wasn't shiny.
   b. Their kitchen floor is dull now.

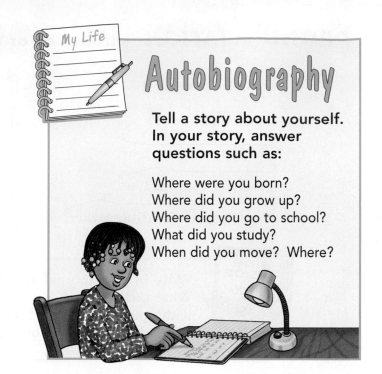

Autobiography

Tell a story about yourself. In your story, answer questions such as:

Where were you born?
Where did you grow up?
Where did you go to school?
What did you study?
When did you move? Where?

ON YOUR OWN *Do You Remember Your Childhood?*

Yes, { I / he / she / it } was.
{ we / you / they } were.

No, { I / he / she / it } wasn't.
{ we / you / they } weren't.

Yes, { I / he / she / it / we / you / they } did.

No, { I / he / she / it / we / you / they } didn't.

Answer these questions and then ask other students in your class.

1. What did you look like?
   Were you tall? thin? pretty? handsome? cute?
   Did you have curly hair? straight hair? long hair?
   Did you have dimples? freckles?

2. Did you have many friends?
   What did you do with your friends?
   What games did you play?

3. Did you like school?
   Who was your favorite teacher? Why?
   What was your favorite subject? Why?

4. What did you do in your spare time?
   Did you have a hobby?
   Did you play sports?

5. Who was your favorite hero?

Listen. Then say it.

Were you tall?

Did you have long hair?

What did you look like?

Who was your favorite teacher?

Say it. Then listen.

Were you short?

Did you have freckles?

Where did you grow up?

When did you move?

SIDE by SIDE JOURNAL

Write in your journal about your childhood. What did you look like? What did you do with your friends? Did you like school? What did you do in your spare time?

CHAPTER SUMMARY

GRAMMAR

To Be: Past Tense

I He She It	was	
We You They	were	happy.

I He She It	wasn't	
We You They	weren't	tired.

Was	I he she it	
Were	we you they	late?

Yes,	I he she it	was.
	we you they	were.

No,	I he she it	wasn't.
	we you they	weren't.

KEY VOCABULARY

ADJECTIVES

beautiful	enormous	heavy	shiny	ugly
clean	exciting	hungry	sick	uncomfortable
comfortable	full	late	thin	
dirty	good	poor	thirsty	
dull	happy	quiet	tiny	
energetic	healthy	sad	tired	

VERBS RELATED TO LIFE EVENTS

arrive	live
be born	move
begin – began	study
grow up – grew up	work

Advertisements

How do advertisers sell their products?

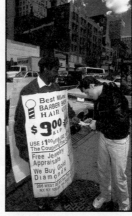

Advertisements are everywhere! They are on television, on the radio, and in newspapers and magazines. Ads are also on billboards, on buses and trains, and even in movie theaters. People get advertisements in their mail. There are also a lot of advertisements on the Internet.

Advertisements are sometimes in unusual places—in elevators, on top of taxis, and in public bathrooms. People sometimes carry signs with ads on the street, and small airplanes sometimes carry signs in the sky. Advertisers are always looking for new places for their ads.

FACT FILE

Countries Where Advertisers Spend the Most Money	United States	Brazil
	Japan	Italy
	United Kingdom	Australia
	Germany	Canada
	France	Korea

LISTENING

And Now a Word From Our Sponsors!

_d_ ❶ Dazzle	**a.**	floor wax
___ ❷ Shiny-Time	**b.**	dog shampoo
___ ❸ Energy Plus	**c.**	throat lozenges
___ ❹ Lucky Lemon Drops	**d.**	toothpaste
___ ❺ K-9 Shine	**e.**	vitamins

Shopping

People around the world buy things in different ways.

This person is shopping in a store.

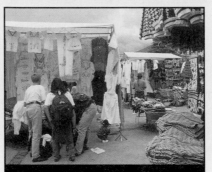

These people are buying things at an outdoor market.

This person is ordering something from a catalog over the telephone.

This person is buying something from a home shopping channel on TV.

These people are looking for things at a yard sale.

This person is shopping on the Internet.

What are the ways people buy things in different countries you know?

Global Exchange

TedG: I had a very busy day today. I got up at 6:30, took a shower, ate breakfast, and went to school. In my English class this morning, I read a long story, and I wrote my autobiography. I didn't have time for lunch because I had to meet with my Spanish teacher. After I met with her, I went to math class. We had a big test today. It was very difficult! After school, I went to a basketball game. Then I went home, did some homework, had dinner, and did some more homework. How about you? What did you do today?

Send a message to a keypal. Tell about what you did today.

What Are They Saying?

Listening Scripts

Chapter 9 – Page 84

Listen and choose the correct answer.

1. My brother lives in Chicago.
2. My name is Peter. I work in an office.
3. This is my friend Carla. She speaks Italian.
4. My sister drives a bus in Chicago.
5. We read the newspaper every day.
6. My parents visit their friends every weekend.
7. Charlie cooks in a Greek restaurant.
8. My brother and I paint houses.
9. My friend Betty calls me every day.
10. My parents usually shop at the mall.

Chapter 10 – Page 93

WHAT'S THE WORD?

Listen and choose the word you hear.

1. Do you work on Monday?
2. Does your daughter go to this school?
3. We do a different activity every Sunday.
4. Larry doesn't play a sport.
5. We don't go to Stanley's Restaurant.
6. Sally goes to a health club every week.
7. She baby-sits for her neighbors every Thursday.
8. They go to work every morning.

WHAT'S THE ANSWER?

Listen and choose the correct response.

1. Do you speak Korean?
2. Does Mrs. Wilson go to Stanley's Restaurant?
3. Does your sister live in Los Angeles?
4. Do you and your brother clean the house together?
5. Does your husband like American food?
6. Do you go to school on the weekend?
7. Do you and your friends play tennis?
8. Does your cousin live in this neighborhood?

***Side by Side* Gazette – Page 98**

You're calling the International Cafe! Listen to the recorded announcement. Match the day of the week and the kind of entertainment.

Hello! This is the International Cafe—your special place for wonderful entertainment every day of the week! Every day the International Cafe presents a different kind of entertainment. On Monday, Antonio Bello plays Italian classical music. On Tuesday, Miguel Garcia reads Spanish poetry. On Wednesday, Amanda Silva sings Brazilian jazz. On Thursday, Nina Markova reads Russian short stories. On Friday, Hiroshi Tanaka plays Japanese rock music. On Saturday, Rita Rivera sings Mexican popular music. And on Sunday, Slim Wilkins sings American country music. So come to the International Cafe—your special place for wonderful entertainment . . . every day of the week!

Chapter 11 – Page 105

Listen to the conversations. Who and what are they talking about?

1. A. How often do you visit him?
   B. I visit him every week.
2. A. How often do you wash them?
   B. I wash them every year.
3. A. Do you write to her very often?
   B. I write to her every month.
4. A. Is it broken?
   B. Yes. I'm fixing it now.
5. A. How often do you see them?
   B. I see them every day.

6. A. How often do you use it?
   B. I use it all the time.
7. A. When does he wash it?
   B. He washes it every Sunday.
8. A. Do you see him very often?
   B. No. I rarely see him.
9. A. Do you study with them very often?
   B. Yes. I study with them all the time.

Chapter 12 – Page 112

Listen and choose the correct answer.

1. What are you doing?
2. What does the office assistant do?
3. What's the receptionist doing?
4. Is he tired?
5. What do you do when you're scared?
6. Where do you usually study?

***Side by Side* Gazette – Page 115**

Listen to these news reports. Match the news and the city.

A. You're listening to WBOS in Boston. And now here's Randy Ryan with today's news.
B. Good morning. Well, the people in Boston who usually take the subway to work aren't taking it today. There's a big problem with the subway system in Boston.

A. You're listening to KSAC in Sacramento. And now here's Jessica Chen with the morning news.
B. Good morning. The big news here in Sacramento is the traffic! Sacramento police officers are on strike today, and nobody is directing traffic. There are traffic problems all around the city!

A. This is WCHI in Chicago. And now here's Mike Maxwell with today's news.
B. Good morning. It's snowing very hard in Chicago right now. As a result, the streets of the city are empty. People aren't walking or driving to work. There aren't any trucks or buses on the street. And mail carriers aren't delivering the mail.

A. You're listening to CTOR in Toronto. And now here's Mark Mitchell with today's news.
B. It's a quiet Tuesday morning in Toronto. There aren't any bad traffic problems right now, and there aren't any problems with the subway system or the buses.

A. You're listening to WMIA in Miami. And now here's today's news.
B. Good morning. This is Rita Rodriguez with the news. The children of Miami who usually take school buses to school aren't taking them this morning. The men and women who drive the school buses are on strike. Some children are walking to school today. Many students are staying home.

Chapter 13 – Page 121

CAN OR CAN'T?

Listen and choose the word you hear.

1. I can speak Spanish.
2. He can't paint.
3. She can type.
4. We can't build things.
5. They can use tools.
6. We can't operate equipment.

Listen and choose what each person can do.

1. He can't file. He can type.
2. They can cook. They can't bake.
3. She can repair locks. She can't repair stoves.
4. I can't drive a truck. I can drive a bus.
5. He can teach French. He can't teach English.
6. We can take inventory. We can't paint.

Chapter 14 – Page 132

Listen and choose the words you hear.

1. A. When are you going to buy a computer?
   B. Tomorrow.
2. A. When are your neighbors going to move?
   B. Next November.
3. A. When are you going to visit me?
   B. Next month.
4. A. When are you going to do your laundry?
   B. This evening.
5. A. When are you going to begin your vacation?
   B. This Sunday.
6. A. When are we going to go to the concert?
   B. This Thursday.
7. A. When are you going to wash the windows?
   B. This afternoon.
8. A. When is she going to get her driver's license?
   B. Next week.
9. A. When is your daughter going to finish college?
   B. Next winter.
10. A. When is the landlord going to fix the kitchen sink?
    B. At once.

Side by Side Gazette – Page 140

Listen and match the theaters and the movies.

Thank you for calling the Multiplex Cinema! The Multiplex Cinema has five theaters with the best movies in town!

Now showing in Theater One: *The Spanish Dancer,* a film from Spain about the life of the famous dancer Carlos Montero. Show times are at one fifteen, three thirty, and seven o'clock.

Now showing in Theater Two: *When Are You Going to Call the Plumber*?, starring Julie Richards and Harry Grant. In this comedy, a husband and wife have a lot of problems in their new house. Show times are at two thirty, four forty-five, and seven fifteen.

Now showing in Theater Three: *The Fortune Teller*. In this film from Brazil, a woman tells people all the things that are going to happen in their lives. Show times are at five o'clock, seven forty-five, and ten fifteen.

Now showing in Theater Four: *The Time Zone Machine*, the exciting new science fiction movie. Professor Stanley Carrington's new machine can send people to different time zones around the world. Show times are at five fifteen, eight o'clock, and ten thirty. There's also a special show at midnight.

Now showing in Theater Five: *Tomorrow Is Right Now*. In this new drama, a truck driver from Australia falls in love with a businesswoman from Paris. Where are they going to live, and what are they going to tell their friends? See it and find out! Show times are at six o'clock, eight thirty, and ten forty-five.

The Multiplex Cinema is on Harrison Avenue, across from the shopping mall. So come and see a movie at the Multiplex Cinema. You're going to have a good time! Thank you, and have a nice day!

Chapter 15 – Page 147

Listen and choose the word you hear.

1. We plant flowers in our garden in the spring.
2. I worked at the office all day.
3. They studied English all morning.
4. Mr. and Mrs. Jones sit in their living room all day.
5. They drank lemonade all summer.
6. I waited for the bus all morning.
7. They finish their work at five o'clock.
8. We invited our friends to the party.
9. I eat cheese and crackers.
10. She cleaned her apartment all afternoon.
11. We wash our clothes at the laundromat.
12. He watched TV all evening.

Chapter 16 – Page 155

Listen and put a check next to all the things these people did today.

Carla got up early this morning. She took a shower, she had breakfast, and she took the subway to work. She didn't have lunch today. She left work at five thirty, and she met her mother at six o'clock. They had dinner at a restaurant. Then they saw a movie.

Brian had a busy day today. This morning he fixed his car. Then he cleaned his yard. This afternoon he planted flowers, and then he washed his windows. This evening he read the newspaper, and he wrote to his brother. Then he took a bath.

Chapter 17 – Page 163

Listen and choose the correct answer.

1. Before we bought Captain Crispy Cereal, we were always sick. Now we're always healthy.
2. We bought new chairs for our living room because our old chairs were very uncomfortable. We love our new chairs. They're VERY comfortable.
3. My daughter Lucy didn't finish her milk this morning. She wasn't very thirsty.
4. Fred was very upset this morning. He was late for the bus, and he didn't get to work on time.
5. Hmm. Where are Peter and Mary? They were at work yesterday, but they aren't here today.
6. Our kitchen floor was very dull. Our neighbors recommended Sparkle Floor Wax, and now our kitchen floor isn't dull any more. It's shiny!

Side by Side Gazette – Page 165

Listen and match the products.

ANNOUNCER: And now a word from our sponsors.
WOMAN: I had a problem with my teeth. They were very yellow, and I was upset. I went to my dentist, and she recommended Dazzle. So I went to the store and I bought some. Now I brush my teeth with Dazzle every day. My teeth aren't yellow any more. They're white. They're VERY white! Thank you, Dazzle!
ANNOUNCER: Are YOUR teeth yellow? Try Dazzle today!

TED: Bob! This kitchen floor is beautiful!
BOB: Thanks, Ted.
TED: Is it new?
BOB: Oh, no! This is my old kitchen floor.
TED: But it's so shiny!
BOB: That's right, Ted. It IS shiny, because I bought Shiny-Time!
TED: Shiny-Time?
BOB: Yes. Shiny-Time!
ANNOUNCER: That's right, Ted. YOU can have a shiny kitchen floor, too. Use Shiny-Time . . . every time!

WOMAN: Alan? What's the matter?

MAN: I don't know. I jog all the time, but today I'm really tired. Tell me, Julie, you're NEVER tired. You're always energetic. How do you do it?

WOMAN: Energy Plus!

MAN: Energy Plus?

WOMAN: Yes, Alan, Energy Plus! Before I bought Energy Plus, I was always tired like you. But now I'm energetic all the time!

ANNOUNCER: Tired? Try Energy Plus today! You can find it in supermarkets and drug stores everywhere.

PRESIDENT: Thank you. Thank you very much.

ASSISTANT: That was excellent, Mr. President.

PRESIDENT: Thank you, Ron. You know, I have a terrible sore throat.

ASSISTANT: I can hear that, Mr. President. Here. Try one of these.

PRESIDENT: What are they?

ASSISTANT: Lucky Lemon Drops.

PRESIDENT: Lucky Lemon Drops?

ASSISTANT: Yes, Mr. President. They're really good for a sore throat.

PRESIDENT: Thanks, Ron.

ANNOUNCER: Lucky Lemon Drops. They're good for the president! They're good for you!

WOMAN: My dog's fur was dull. It was VERY dull, and my dog was very sad. Then I bought K-9 Shine! Yes, K-9 Shine. I washed my dog with K-9 Shine, and now his fur is shiny! It's very shiny, and my dog is very happy!

ANNOUNCER: Try K-9 Shine today! YOUR dog's fur can be shiny, too!

Thematic Glossary

Ailments 141

backache
cold
cough
earache
fever
headache
sore throat
stomachache
toothache

Days of the Week 87

Sunday
Monday
Tuesday
Wednesday
Thursday
Friday
Saturday

Describing Feelings and Emotions

annoyed 124
depressed 122
embarrassed 107
hungry 107
nervous 107
scared 107

sick 107
thirsty 107

Describing People and Things

active 90
athletic 90
bad 112
blond 102
closed 165
comfortable 157
cute 163
dark 165
dry 165
dull 157
energetic 112
enormous 157
exciting 162
fancy 165
fast 165
full 157
healthy 157
high 165
late 161
light 165
long 165
low 165
messy 165
neat 165

open 165
outgoing 94
plain 165
popular 94
shiny 157
shy 94
slow 165
tiny 157
uncomfortable 157
wet 165

Everyday Activities

baby-sit 87
call 79
comb *my* hair 97
deliver 113
do *yoga* 87
drive 79
get dressed 97
get up 97
go 89
go *dancing* 87
go to bed 97
go to school 97
go to work 97
jog 87
see 87
sell 79
shave 135
skate 118

ski 118
speak 79
sweep 111
take a bath 97
take a shower 97
take a taxi 115
take the bus 113
take the subway 115
take the train 115
type 112
visit 79
walk 111
work 79

Months of the Year 127

January
February
March
April
May
June
July
August
September
October
November
December

Occupations

architect 139
baker 117
carpenter 139
cashier 139
chef 117
construction worker 117
custodian 112
dancer 117
farmer 139
journalist 103
lawyer 139
mail carrier 113
mechanic 117
office assistant 112
painter 139
pilot 139
police officer 113
receptionist 112
salesperson 117
secretary 117
singer 117
translator 139
truck driver 117
waiter 139
waitress 139

Seasons 127

spring
summer
fall/autumn
winter

Skills

build 115
file 120
operate 120
repair 120
sort the mail 112
speak *Spanish* 79
take inventory 120
type 112
use 111

Time Expressions

afternoon 92
evening 92
month 99
morning 92
week 92
weekend 83

Cardinal Numbers

1	one	20	twenty
2	two	21	twenty-one
3	three	22	twenty-two
4	four		.
5	five		.
6	six	29	twenty-nine
7	seven	30	thirty
8	eight	40	forty
9	nine	50	fifty
10	ten	60	sixty
11	eleven	70	seventy
12	twelve	80	eighty
13	thirteen	90	ninety
14	fourteen	100	one hundred
15	fifteen	200	two hundred
16	sixteen		.
17	seventeen		.
18	eighteen	900	nine hundred
19	nineteen	1,000	one thousand
		2,000	two thousand
			.
		10,000	ten thousand
		100,000	one hundred thousand
		1,000,000	one million

Irregular Verbs: Past Tense

be	was
begin	began
buy	bought
do	did
drink	drank
drive	drove
eat	ate
forget	forgot
get	got
go	went
grow	grew
have	had
make	made
meet	met
read	read
ride	rode
see	saw
sing	sang
sit	sat
steal	stole
take	took
write	wrote

Index

ACTIVITY WORKBOOK

SIDE by SIDE

THIRD EDITION

Steven J. Molinsky
Bill Bliss

with

Carolyn Graham • Peter S. Bliss

Contributing Authors

Dorothy Lynde • Elizabeth Handley

Longman

BOOK 1B

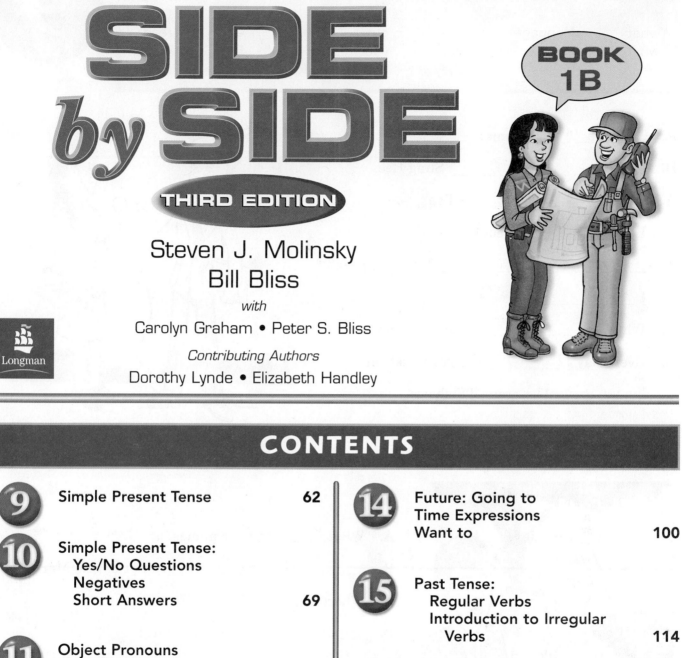

CONTENTS

what	language	we	our	is	eat	read
what's	name	you	your	are	live	watch
where	names	they	their	do	sing	speak

A.   __What's__ 1 your name?

B.   My _____ 2 _____ 3 Sung Hee.

A.   Where _____ 4 _____ 5 live?

B.   I _____ 6 in Seoul.

A.   _____ 7 _____ 8 do you speak?

B.   I _____ 9 Korean.

A.   What _____ 10 _____ 11 do every day?

B.   Every day I _____ 12 Korean food, and

   I _____ 13 Korean TV shows.

A.   What _____ 14 your names?

B.   _____ 15 _____ 16 are Carlos and Maria.

A.   Where _____ 17 _____ 18 live?

B.   _____ 19 _____ 20 in Madrid.

A.   _____ 21 language _____ 22 _____ 23 speak?

B.   We _____ 24 Spanish.

A.   What _____ 25 you _____ 26 every day?

B.   Every day _____ 27 _____ 28 Spanish songs,

   and we _____ 29 Spanish newspapers.

A. _____ <u>30</u> _____ <u>31</u> their names?

B. _____ <u>32</u> _____ <u>33</u> _____ <u>34</u>
Yuko and Toshi.

A. _____ <u>35</u> _____ <u>36</u> they live?

B. _____ <u>37</u> _____ <u>38</u> in Kyoto.

A. _____ <u>39</u> _____ <u>40</u> _____ <u>41</u>
_____ <u>42</u> speak?

B. They _____ <u>43</u> Japanese.

A. What _____ <u>44</u> they _____ <u>45</u> every day?

B. Every day _____ <u>46</u> _____ <u>47</u> Japanese food,

and _____ <u>48</u> _____ <u>49</u> Japanese TV shows.

B LISTENING

Listen and choose the correct response.

1. **(a.)** My name is Kenji.
   b. I live in Tokyo.

2. a. They speak Italian.
   b. I speak Italian.

3. a. They watch Russian TV shows.
   b. I watch Russian TV shows.

4. a. We live in Seoul.
   b. They live in Seoul.

5. a. We eat French food.
   b. We speak French.

6. a. They live in Madrid.
   b. We sing Spanish songs.

C PEOPLE AROUND THE WORLD

My name is Jane. I live in Montreal. Every day I play the piano, and I listen to Canadian music.

1. What's her name? _____ Her name is Jane. _____

2. Where does she live? _____

3. What does she do every day? _____

(continued)

My name is Omar. I live in Cairo. I speak Arabic. Every day I eat Egyptian food, and I read Egyptian newspapers.

4. _____ ?　His name is Omar.

5. _____ ?　He lives in Cairo.

6. What language does he speak?　_____

7. What _____ every day?　He _____ Egyptian food, and _____

_____ .

My name is Sonia. I live in Sao Paolo. I speak Portuguese. Every day I do exercises, and I play soccer.

8. What's her name?　_____

9. _____ she live?　_____

10. What language _____ ?　_____

11. What _____ every day?　_____

_____

D　WRITE ABOUT YOURSELF

1. What's your name?　..

2. Where do you live?　..

3. What language do you speak?　..

4. What do you do every day?　..

....

Listen. Then clap and practice.

A.   What's his   name?

B.   His name is   Joe.

A.   Where does he live?

B.   In Mexico.

A.   What's his   name?

B.   His name is   Lance.

A.   Where does he live?

B.   He lives in   France.

A.   What's her   name?

B.   Her name is   Anne.

A.   Where does she live?

B.   She lives in   Japan.

A.   What's her   name?

B.   Her name is Anastasia.

A.   Where does she live?

B.   She lives in   Malaysia.

A.   What's her   name?

B.   Her name is   Denise.

A.   Where does she live?

B.   She lives in   Greece.

A.   What's her   name?

B.   Her name is   Maria.

A.   Where does she live?

B.   She lives in   Korea.

Activity Workbook   **65**

F EDUARDO'S FAMILY

Fill in the correct form of the verb.

clean	cook	do	live	play	read	shop	speak	work
cleans	cooks	does	lives	plays	reads	shops	speaks	works

My name is Eduardo. I _____live_____ ¹ in Rio de Janeiro. I _____ ² English and

Portuguese. My wife's name is Sonia. She _____ ³ English, Portuguese, and Spanish. Our

children, Fernando and Claudio, also _____ ⁴ English and Portuguese. At school they

_____ ⁵ English and Portuguese books.

We _____ ⁶ in a large apartment. Every day my wife _____ ⁷ the newspaper

and _____ ⁸ in a bank. I _____ ⁹ breakfast and _____ ¹⁰ in an office.

Every weekend we _____ ¹¹ our apartment. I also _____ ¹² at the supermarket.

Fernando _____ ¹³ soccer with his friends, and Claudio and I _____ ¹⁴ basketball.

What languages _____ ¹⁵ YOU speak? What do YOU _____ ¹⁶ every day?

G LISTENING

Listen and circle the word you hear.

1. (live)   lives   4. listen   listens   7. sing   sings

2. do   does   5. watch   watches   8. eat   eats

3. do   does   6. eat   eats   9. read   reads

WHAT'S THE WORD?

| do does | cook | drive | live | paint | sell |

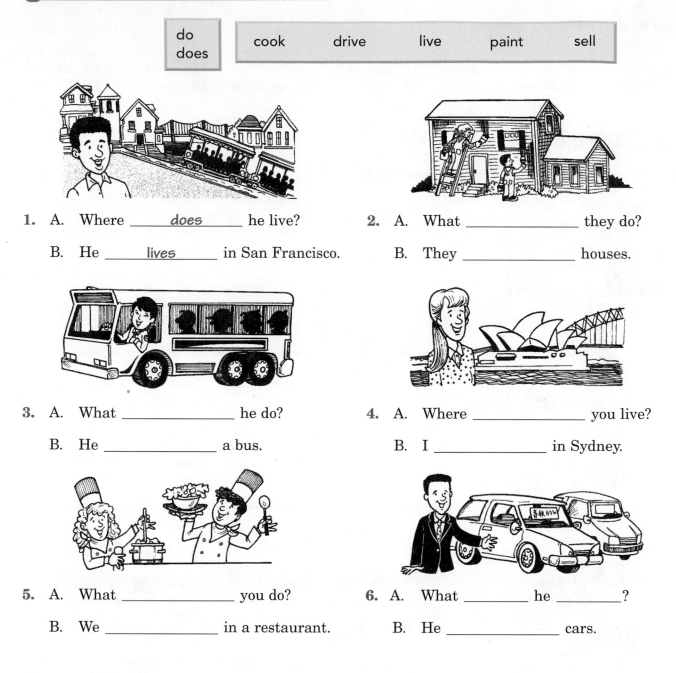

1. A. Where _____does_____ he live?

   B. He _____lives_____ in San Francisco.

2. A. What _____ they do?

   B. They _____ houses.

3. A. What _____ he do?

   B. He _____ a bus.

4. A. Where _____ you live?

   B. I _____ in Sydney.

5. A. What _____ you do?

   B. We _____ in a restaurant.

6. A. What _____ he _____?

   B. He _____ cars.

I **WHAT'S THE DIFFERENCE?**

1. I drive a bus. My friend Carla _____drives_____ a taxi.

2. We _____ in a bank. They work in an office.

3. Victor _____ the violin. His children play the piano.

4. I sell cars. My wife _____ computers.

5. I paint houses. My brother _____ pictures.

6. We live in Los Angeles. Our son _____ in London.

Listen to each word and then say it.

1. chair	4. Chen	7. church	10. children	13. Sharp	16. Shirley	19. short
2. bench	5. kitchen	8. cheap	11. Richard	14. shirt	17. washing	20. English
3. Charlie	6. Chinese	9. watch	12. shoes	15. machine	18. station	21. French

K LOUD AND CLEAR Ch! Sh!

Fill in the words. Then read the sentences aloud.

chair	Charlie	kitchen	Chinese

1. ___Charlie___ is sitting in a ___chair___ in his

_____ and eating _____ food.

Shirley	short	shoes

2. _____ isn't _____ in her new

_____.

watch	Richard	cheap	French

3. _____ is looking for a _____

_____ _____.

shirt	washing	washing machine

4. He's _____ his _____ in his

_____ _____.

bench	children	Chen	church

5. Mr. _____ and his _____ are sitting

on a _____ in front of the _____.

Sharp	station	English

6. Mr. _____ is in London at an _____

train _____.

A WHAT'S THE DAY?

1. Monday _____Tuesday_____ Wednesday

2. Friday _____ Sunday

3. Tuesday _____ Thursday

4. Saturday _____ Monday

5. Thursday _____ Saturday

6. Sunday _____ Tuesday

B WHAT ARE THEY SAYING?

Yes, { he / she / it } does.   No, { he / she / it } doesn't.

what kind of
when

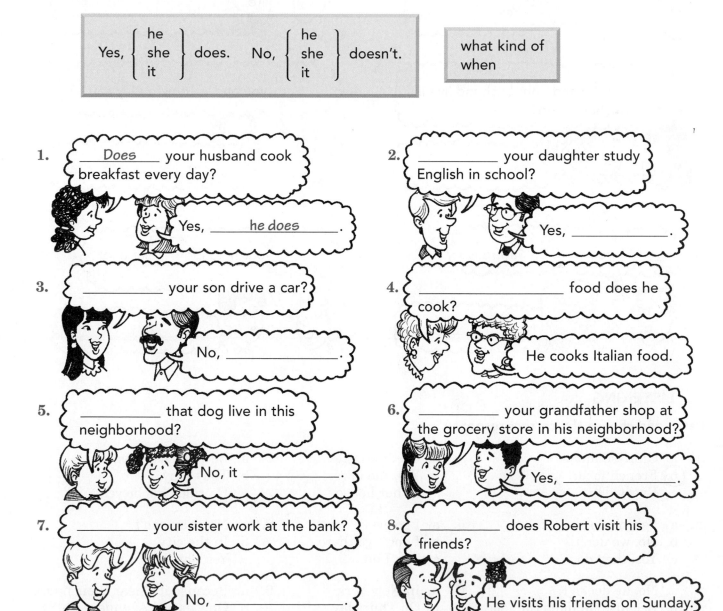

1. ____Does____ your husband cook breakfast every day?

Yes, _____he does_____.

2. _____ your daughter study English in school?

Yes, _____.

3. _____ your son drive a car?

No, _____.

4. _____ food does he cook?

He cooks Italian food.

5. _____ that dog live in this neighborhood?

No, it _____.

6. _____ your grandfather shop at the grocery store in his neighborhood?

Yes, _____.

7. _____ your sister work at the bank?

No, _____.

8. _____ does Robert visit his friends?

He visits his friends on Sunday.

Yes, { I / we / you / they } do.   No, { I / we / you / they } don't.

1. ___Do___ you sing in the shower?

    Yes, ___I do___.

2. _____ your children speak French?

    No, _____.

3. _____ you and your husband live in this neighborhood?

    Yes, _____.

4. _____ you and your wife play cards?

    No, _____.

5. _____ you work on Saturday?

    No, _____.

6. _____ your neighbors make a lot of noise?

    Yes, _____.

D LISTENING

Listen and choose the correct response.

1. a. Chinese music.
    b. French food.
    c. Every day.

2. a. Yes, he does.
    b. No, we don't.
    c. Yes, they do.

3. a. No, he doesn't.
    b. Because he likes the food.
    c. On Wednesday.

4. a. On Sunday.
    b. Yes, she does.
    c. In her house.

5. a. I go every day.
    b. I don't go there.
    c. Yes, I do.

6. a. In New York.
    b. On Thursday.
    c. They don't go there.

7. a. Because it's open.
    b. They play.
    c. He rides his bicycle.

8. a. No, they don't.
    b. In the city.
    c. Yes, she does.

9. a. Because it's near their house.
    b. On Central Avenue.
    c. Yes, they do.

E YES AND NO

1. My husband cooks Italian food. He __doesn't__ __cook__ Thai food.

2. Linda drives a taxi. She _____ _____ a bus.

3. Our children play the piano. They _____ _____ the guitar.

4. I work on Saturday. I _____ _____ on Sunday.

5. Tom lives in an apartment. He _____ _____ in a house.

6. My wife and I exercise in the park. We _____ _____ in a health club.

7. Every Saturday Mrs. Roberts _____ to the library. She doesn't go to the mall.

8. I _____ in large supermarkets. I don't shop in small grocery stores.

9. My mother _____ stockings. She doesn't wear socks.

10. Omar _____ Arabic. He doesn't speak Spanish.

11. Harry sings in the shower. He _____ _____ in the jacuzzi.

F WHAT'S THE WORD?

do	does

1. Where __do__ they live?

2. When _____ your daughter do her homework?

3. What kind of books _____ you read?

4. Why _____ he call you every day?

5. What languages _____ they speak?

6. Where _____ your husband work?

7. _____ you visit your friends every week?

8. _____ he go to Stanley's Restaurant?

9. When _____ you go to the supermarket?

10. _____ your children wash the dishes?

11. What kind of music _____ she listen to?

12. What _____ he sell?

13. Why _____ they cry at weddings?

G WRITE ABOUT YOURSELF

1. I like _____   I don't like _____

2. I play _____   I don't play _____

3. I speak _____   I don't speak _____

4. I eat _____   I don't eat _____

5. I cook _____   I don't cook _____

H YES OR NO?

1. Does Kathy take karate lessons?

Yes, she does.

2. Do Jim and Tom play tennis on Sunday?

No, they don't. They play volleyball.

3. Do you and Harry go dancing on Friday?

4. Does Miguel play in the orchestra?

5. Do you see a movie every weekend?

6. Do Mr. and Mrs. Kim go to a health club?

7. Does Richard jog in the park?

8. Do you and your wife watch TV every day?

I LISTENING 🎞️💿

Listen and choose the correct response.

1. a. Yes, they do.
    ⓑ. Yes, I do.

2. a. Yes, he does.
    b. Yes, I do.

3. a. No, he doesn't.
    b. No, they don't.

4. a. No, she doesn't.
    b. No, I don't.

5. a. Yes, we do.
    b. Yes, he does.

6. a. Yes, we do.
    b. No, they don't.

7. a. No, I don't.
    b. Yes, he does.

8. a. Yes, they do.
    b. Yes, he does.

9. a. No, we don't.
    b. No, they don't.

J GrammarRap: *They Do, They Don't*

Listen. Then clap and practice.

Does he	Yes he	No he

A.   Does he eat French   bread?

B.   Yes, he   does.

A.   Does she like Swiss   cheese?

B.   Yes, she   does.

A.   Do they cook Greek   food?

B.   Yes, they   do.

A. Do they speak   Chinese?

B.   Yes, they   do.

All.   He eats French   bread.

    She likes Swiss   cheese.

    They cook Greek   food.

  And they speak   Chinese.

A. Does he read the   paper?

B.   No, he   doesn't.

A. Does she watch   TV?

B.   No, she   doesn't.

A. Do they go to   movies?

B.   No, they   don't.

A. Do they drink iced   tea?

B.   No, they   don't.

All.   He doesn't read the paper.

    She doesn't watch   TV.

    They don't go to   movies.

  And they don't drink   tea.

K A LETTER TO A PEN PAL

Read and practice.

Wednesday

Dear Peter,

My family and I live in San Juan. We speak Spanish. My mother is a music teacher. She plays the violin and the piano. My father works in an office.

My brother Ramon and I go to school every day. We study history, English, Spanish, science, and mathematics. My favorite school subject is science. I don't like history, but I like mathematics.

Do you like sports? Every day at school I play soccer. On Saturday I swim. What sports do you play? What kind of music do you like? I like rock music and country music very much, but I don't like jazz. What kind of movies do you like? I like adventure movies and comedies. I think science fiction movies are terrible.

Tell me about your family and your school.

Your friend,
Maria

L YOUR LETTER TO A PEN PAL

history
English
mathematics
science
music

baseball
football
hockey
golf
tennis
soccer

cartoons
dramas
comedies
westerns
adventure movies
science fiction
    movies

classical music
jazz
popular music
rock music
country music

Dear ....,

My family and I live in .... We speak

.... At school, I study ....,

...................................., and .... My favorite subject is

.... I don't like ....

What sports do you play? I play .... and

.... I think .... is wonderful. I don't

like ....

What kind of movies do you like? I like .... and

....

My favorite kind of music is ...., and I like

.... I don't listen to ....

Tell me about your school and your city.

Your friend,

....

✓ CHECK-UP TEST: Chapters 9-10

A. Circle the correct answers.

Ex. We (live) / lives in Tokyo.

1. Tom play / plays in the park.

2. My wife and I shop / shops on Monday.

3. She don't / doesn't work on Saturday.

4. Where do / does your cousins live?

5. We stays / stay home every Sunday.

6. What activities do / does she do?

B. Fill in the blanks.

Ex. ___What___ is your address?

1. _____ does he live?

2. _____ kind of food do you like?

3. _____ Patty baby-sit for her neighbors?

4. _____ do you eat at that restaurant?
   Because we like the food.

5. _____ does Julie go to a health club?
   On Monday.

6. _____ does your family do on Sunday?

C. Fill in the blanks.

Mrs. Davis _____ [1] in Dallas. She's a very active person. She _____ [2] exercises every day. On Monday she _____ [3] her apartment, on Wednesday she _____ [4] tennis, on Friday she _____ [5] a karate lesson, on Saturday she _____ [6] her bicycle in the park, and on Sunday she _____ [7] to a museum and _____ [8] lunch in a restaurant.

D. Listen and choose the correct response.

Ex. a. We go to school.
    (b.) They work in an office.
    c. They're shy.

1. a. Yes, we do.
   b. We like dramas.
   c. On Thursday.

2. a. In a restaurant.
   b. Because we like it.
   c. Every day.

3. a. Yes, they do.
   b. Yes, he does.
   c. In Puerto Rico.

4. a. Short stories.
   b. News programs.
   c. I like golf.

5. a. Yes, they do.
   b. Because it's convenient.
   c. On Center Street.

A WHAT ARE THEY SAYING?

me	us
him	you
her	them
it	

1. Do you like me?
Of course I like __you__.

2. Do you like your neighbors?
Of course I like _____.

3. Do you like Helen?
Of course I like _____.

4. Do you like George?
Of course I like _____.

5. Do you like videos?
Of course I like _____.

6. Do you like English?
Of course I like _____.

7. Do your friends like you?
Of course they like _____.

8. Do you like your new apartment?
Of course I like _____.

9. Does your dog like you?
Of course he likes _____.

B WHAT'S THE WORD?

it	her	him	them

1. She washes ___it___ every morning.

2. I think about _____ all the time.

3. We visit _____ every weekend.

4. I talk to _____ every night.

5. He uses _____ every day.

6. We feed _____ every afternoon.

C LISTENING

Listen and put a check (✓) under the correct picture.

1. _____ ✔

2. _____ _____

3. _____ _____

4. _____ _____

5. _____ _____

6. _____ _____

D WRITE ABOUT YOURSELF

1. I .... every day.

2. I .... every week.

3. I .... every month.

4. I .... every year.

5. I .... every weekend.

6. I .... every Sunday.

7. I .... every morning.

8. I .... all the time.

E WRITE IT AND SAY IT

Write the correct form of the word in parentheses and then say the sentence.

1. Carol sometimes (eat) __eats__ Thai food.

2. My neighbor's dog always (bark) _____ in the afternoon.

3. My son never (clean) _____ his bedroom.

4. Ray always (wash) _____ his car on the weekend.

5. My brother sometimes (jog) _____ at night.

6. Amy usually (read) _____ poetry.

7. My mother rarely (shop) _____ at the grocery store around the corner.

8. Dan sometimes (watch) _____ videos on Saturday.

9. Omar usually (speak) _____ English at work.

10. Patty usually (play) _____ tennis in the park on Saturday.

F MATCHING

__c__ 1. Walter always washes his car on Sunday.

____ 2. Jonathan never cooks dinner.

____ 3. Carla rarely watches comedies.

____ 4. My grandmother rarely speaks English.

____ 5. Richard usually jogs in the morning.

____ 6. Larry never writes letters.

____ 7. Nancy rarely studies at home.

____ 8. Jane always fixes her computer.

a. She usually watches dramas.

b. He rarely jogs at night.

c. He never washes it during the week.

d. She usually studies in the library.

e. He always eats in a restaurant.

f. He always writes e-mail messages.

g. She usually speaks Spanish.

h. She never calls a repairperson.

G LISTENING

Listen and choose the correct answer.

1. a. He usually washes it.
   b. He never washes it.

2. a. My husband sometimes cooks.
   b. My husband never cooks.

3. a. My neighbors are quiet.
   b. My neighbors are noisy.

4. a. They usually speak Spanish.
   b. They usually speak English.

5. a. Jane is shy.
   b. Jane is outgoing.

6. a. I usually study at home.
   b. I usually study in the library.

| always | usually | sometimes | rarely | never |

1. I .... wear glasses.
2. I .... eat Italian food.
3. I .... listen to country music.
4. I .... go to English class.
5. I .... watch videos.
6. I .... read poetry.
7. I .... fix my car.
8. I .... visit my grandparents.

9. I .... watch game shows on TV.
10. I .... use a cell phone.
11. I .... clean my apartment.
12. I always ....
13. I usually ....
14. I sometimes ....
15. I rarely ....
16. I never ....

I **GRAMMARRAP:** *I Always Get to Work on Time*

Listen. Then clap and practice.

A.   I always get to   work on time.

    I'm usually here by   eight.

    I sometimes get here   early.

    I never get here   late.

    No, I never get here   late.

B.   He always gets to   work on time.

    He's usually here by   eight.

    He sometimes gets here early.

    He rarely gets here   late.

A.   No! I NEVER get here   late.

B.   Right! He never gets here   late.

have	has

1. Do you ___have___ a bicycle?

2. My daughter _____ curly hair.

3. My parents _____ an old car.

4. Does your son _____ blond hair?

5. Our building _____ a satellite dish.

6. Do you _____ large sunglasses?

7. My sister _____ green eyes.

8. We _____ two dogs and a cat.

K **WHAT ARE THEY SAYING?**

have	has	do	does	don't	doesn't

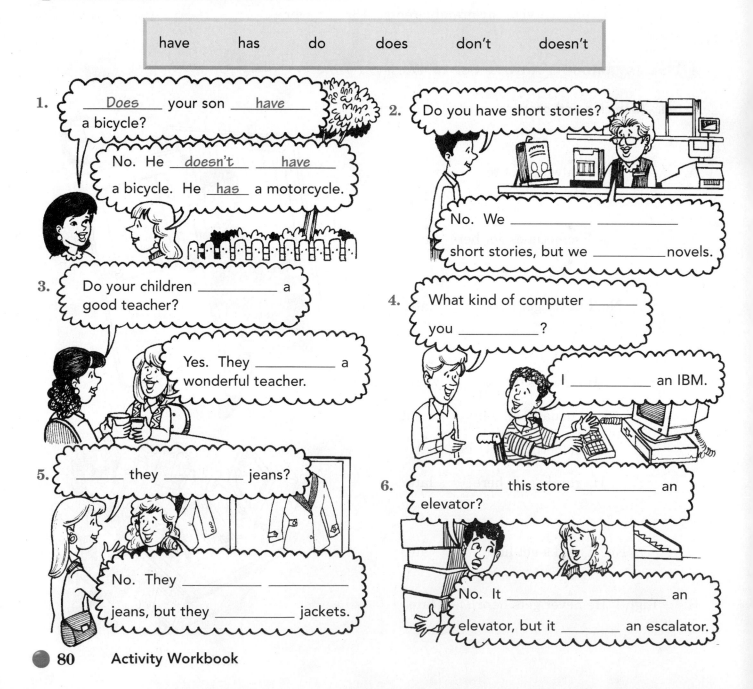

1. ___Does___ your son ___have___ a bicycle?

   No. He ___doesn't___ ___have___ a bicycle. He ___has___ a motorcycle.

2. Do you have short stories?

   No. We _____ _____ short stories, but we _____ novels.

3. Do your children _____ a good teacher?

   Yes. They _____ a wonderful teacher.

4. What kind of computer _____ you _____?

   I _____ an IBM.

5. _____ they _____ jeans?

   No. They _____ _____ jeans, but they _____ jackets.

6. _____ this store _____ an elevator?

   No. It _____ _____ an elevator, but it _____ an escalator.

L WHAT'S THE WORD?

1. Tina doesn't have short hair. She has (long) / curly hair.

2. I don't have straight hair. I have thin / curly hair.

3. My brother isn't tall. He's heavy / short .

4. Albert isn't married. He's curly / single .

5. Your baby boy has beautiful blond eyes / hair .

6. His eyes aren't blue. They're brown / straight .

7. We don't live in the city. We live in the house / suburbs .

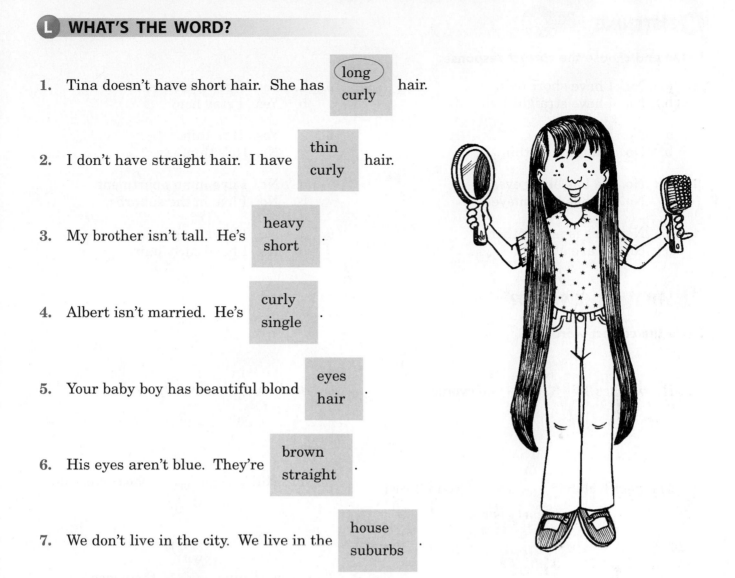

M TWO BROTHERS

My brother and I are very different. I'm tall, and he's _____short_____ 1. I _____ 2 brown

eyes, and he _____ 3 blue eyes. We both _____ 4 brown hair, but I have long, straight

hair, and he has _____ 5, _____ 6 hair. I'm short and heavy. And he's _____ 7 and

_____ 8. I'm a chef, and _____ 9 a doctor. I live in New York. He _____ 10 in San

Diego. I have a small apartment in the city. He _____ 11 a large house _____ 12 the

suburbs. I play tennis. He _____ 13 golf. I play the guitar. He doesn't _____ 14 a musical

instrument. On the weekend, I usually _____ 15 to parties. He doesn't _____ 16 to parties.

He _____ 17 TV and _____ 18 the newspaper.

Listen and choose the correct response.

1. a. No. I have short hair.
   b. No. I have straight hair. *(b circled)*

2. a. No. I'm single.
   b. No. I'm tall and thin.

3. a. No. He has black eyes.
   b. No. He has brown eyes.

4. a. No. This is my mother.
   b. No. I have a sister.

5. a. Yes. I go to parties.
   b. Yes. I stay home.

6. a. Yes. He's thin.
   b. No. He's thin.

7. a. No. I live in an apartment.
   b. No. I live in the suburbs.

8. a. No. I have long hair.
   b. No. I have curly hair.

O WHAT'S THE WORD?

Circle the correct word.

1. He watches TV [at / with / **in**] the evening.

2. The health club is [in / on / between] Main Street.

3. I'm playing a game [on / to / in] my computer.

4. Ann is sleeping [on / in / across] the yard.

5. He always talks [about / to / with] the weather.

6. I'm looking [from / for / to] a striped shirt.

7. Do you live [in / on / at] the suburbs?

8. Do your children go [to / at / in] school every day?

9. Tim is swimming [with / on / at] the beach.

10. My son is wearing a pair [from / for / of] new jeans.

11. Do you go [in / to / at] work [at / in / on] Saturday?

12. I listen [to / at / on] the radio in the morning.

A WHAT'S THE WORD?

angry	embarrassed	hot	nervous	scared	thirsty
cold	happy	hungry	sad	sick	tired

1. Howard is crying. He's _____sad_____.

2. Helen is yawning. She's _____.

3. Sam is perspiring. He's _____.

4. Frank is shouting. He's _____.

5. Mrs. Allen is going to the hospital.

   She's _____.

6. Peter is looking at his paper and smiling.

   He's _____.

7. Ben's cat is eating. It's _____.

8. Irene is shivering. She's _____.

9. Louise is biting her nails.

   She's _____.

10. Jason is covering his eyes.

    He's _____.

11. Pam is drinking milk.

    She's _____.

12. Bobby is blushing.

    He's _____.

1. A. Why are they yawning?

   B. <u> They're yawning because they're </u> tired.

   They always <u> yawn when they're tired </u>.

2. A. Why is she crying?

   B. _____ sad.

   She always _____.

3. A. Why is he shivering?

   B. _____ cold.

   He always _____.

4. A. Why are you perspiring?

   B. _____ hot.

   I always _____.

5. A. Why is she smiling?

   B. _____ happy.

   She always _____.

6. A. Why are they eating?

   B. _____ hungry.

   They always _____.

7. A. Why are you shouting?

   B. _____ angry.

   We always _____.

8. A. Why is he covering his eyes?

   B. _____ scared.

   He always _____.

C GRAMMARRAP: *I Smile When I'm Happy*

Listen. Then clap and practice.

A.   I smile when I'm   happy.

       I frown when I'm   sad.

       I blush when I'm embarrassed.

    And I shout when I'm   mad.

B.   Are you smiling?

A.   Yes. I'm happy.

B.   Are you frowning?

A.   Yes. I'm sad.

B.   Are you blushing?

A.   I'm embarrassed.

B.   Are you shouting?

A.   Yes. I'm mad.

D GRAMMARRAP: *Why Are You Doing That?*

Listen. Then clap and practice.

A.   What's Fran   doing?

B.   She's working   late.

A.   Working   late?

       Why's she doing   that?

B.   It's Monday.

       She always works   late on   Monday.

A.   What are you   doing?

B.   We're playing   cards.

A.   Playing   cards?

       Why are you doing that?

B.   It's Tuesday.

       We always play   cards on   Tuesday.

Activity Workbook   **85**

A. What's Bob doing?

B. He's cooking spaghetti.

A. Cooking spaghetti?

Why's he doing that?

B. It's Wednesday.

He always cooks spaghetti on Wednesday.

A. What's Maria doing?

B. She's dancing.

A. Dancing?

Why's she doing that?

B. It's Thursday.

She always dances on Thursday.

A. What's Gary doing?

B. He's bathing his cat.

A. Bathing his cat?

Why's he doing that?

B. It's Friday.

He always bathes his cat on Friday.

A. What are you doing?

B. I'm _____ing.

A. _____?

Why are you doing that?

B. It's Saturday.

I always _____ on Saturday.

1. A.   My sister is cooking dinner today.

    B.   That's strange! She never ___cooks___ dinner.

2. A.   Our children are studying with a flashlight.

    B.   That's strange! They never _____ with a flashlight.

3. A.   Victor is walking to work today.

    B.   That's strange! He never _____ to work.

4. A.   Ann is brushing her teeth in the kitchen.

    B.   That's strange! She never _____ her teeth in the kitchen.

5. A.   The dog is eating in the dining room today.
    B.   That's strange! It never _____ in the dining room.

6. A.   Nancy and Bob are dancing in the office.
    B.   That's strange! They never _____ in the office.

7. A.   Ruth _____ the carpet today.
    B.   That's strange! She never sweeps the carpet.

8. A.   My parents _____ poetry today.
    B.   That's strange! They never read poetry.

9. A.   _____ a typewriter today.

    B.   That's strange! You never use a typewriter.

10. A.   My cousins _____ in the yard.

    B.   That's strange! They never sleep in the yard.

WHAT'S THE QUESTION?

Choose the correct question word. Then write the question.

What	When	Where	Why	What kind of	How many

1. I'm blushing <u>because I'm embarrassed</u>. _____ *Why are you blushing?* _____

2. They play tennis <u>in the park</u>. _____

3. She reads her e-mail <u>at night</u>. _____

4. I like <u>Brazilian</u> food. _____

5. We have <u>ten</u> cats. _____

6. He's using his <u>cell phone</u>. _____

What	How often	Where	Why	What kind of	How many

7. He watches <u>game</u> shows. _____

8. We call our grandchildren <u>every week</u>. _____

9. They <u>play golf</u> every weekend. _____

10. I'm smiling <u>because I'm happy</u>. _____

11. She's eating <u>in the cafeteria</u> today. _____

12. I'm wearing <u>two</u> sweaters. _____

G **WHICH ONE DOESN'T BELONG?**

1.	her	me	them	we
2.	noisy	usually	sometimes	rarely
3.	does	doesn't	has	don't
4.	angry	yoga	nervous	happy
5.	Wednesday	Why	What	When
6.	smiling	shivering	crying	outgoing
7.	clean	sweep	shy	wash
8.	year	evening	night	afternoon

As you listen to each story, read the sentences and check yes or no.

Jennifer and Jason

1. yes ☐ no ☑   Jennifer and Jason are visiting their father.
2. yes ☐ no ☐   Jennifer and Jason are happy.
3. yes ☐ no ☐   Their grandfather isn't taking them to the park.

Our Boss

4. yes ☐ no ☐   Our boss usually smiles at the office.
5. yes ☐ no ☐   He's happy today.
6. yes ☐ no ☐   Everyone is thinking about the weekend.

On Vacation

7. yes ☐ no ☐   I like vacations.
8. yes ☐ no ☐   When the weather is nice, I watch videos.
9. yes ☐ no ☐   I'm swimming at the beach today because it's cold.

Timmy and His Brother

10. yes ☐ no ☐   Timmy is covering his eyes because he's sad.
11. yes ☐ no ☐   Timmy doesn't like science fiction movies.
12. yes ☐ no ☐   Timmy's brother is scared.

I LOUD AND CLEAR   S! Z!

sorry hospital sick sister Sally	scientist speaking What's experiments

1. __Sally__ is __sorry__ her __sister__ is __sick__ in the __hospital__ .

2. _____ the _____ doing? He's _____ about his new _____ .

always	cousin	Athens	busy	is

3. My _____ in _____

_____ very

_____.

doesn't	Sally's	clothes	husband	closet

4. _____ _____ _____

have any clean _____ in his

_____.

Steven	it's	sweeping	is	because

5. _____ _____ _____

the floor _____ _____ dirty.

Sunday	Mrs.	newspaper	Garcia	reads

6. _____ _____ _____ the

_____ every _____.

zoo	students	sometimes	bus	school

7. The _____ in our

_____ _____ go

to the _____ on the _____.

plays	soccer	friends	Tuesday	son

8. My _____ Sam _____

_____ with his _____

every _____.

✓ CHECK-UP TEST: Chapters 11–12

A. Fill in the blanks.

me	him	her	it	us	you	them

Ex. Do you like this book?
Of course I like _____it_____ .

1. Do you look like your father?
Yes. I look like _____ .

2. When my cats are hungry, I always feed
_____ .

3. Sally rarely plays with her sister, but she's
playing with _____ today.

4. I say "hello" to my boss every day, and he
says "hello" to _____ .

5. We're going to the park. Do you want to go
with _____?

B. Fill in the blanks.

Ex. Betty never talks to her landlord, but
she's ___talking___ to him today.

1. We never feed the birds, but we're
_____ them today.

2. Harriet never _____ to parties, but
she's going to a party today.

3. My children never bake, but they're
_____ today.

4. Tim never _____ his TV, but he's
fixing it today.

5. Amy rarely _____ her kitchen
windows, but she's washing them today.

C. Fill in the blanks.

do	does	is	are

Ex. a. What __do__ you usually do on the
weekend?

b. What __is__ Tina doing today?

1. Why _____ the baby crying?

2. When _____ David and Pam go to the
supermarket?

3. _____ Bob usually dance?

4. Do they work here? Yes, they _____ .

5. _____ your parents cooking lunch?

D. Write the question.

Ex. I'm shivering <u>because I'm cold</u>. (Why?)
_____Why are you shivering?_____

1. They work <u>in a laboratory</u> every day.
(Where?)
_____

2. We get together <u>on Saturday</u>. (When?)
_____

3. He's crying <u>because he's sad</u>. (Why?)
_____

4. She has <u>three</u> children. (How many?)
_____

5. I'm drinking <u>milk</u>. (What?)
_____

E. Listen and choose the correct response.

Ex. ⓐ. They're playing soccer.
b. They play tennis.

1. a. They're delivering mail.
b. They deliver mail.

2. a. We're going to the zoo.
b. We go to the park.

3. a. I'm covering my eyes.
b. I cover my eyes.

4. a. No, I don't.
b. No, I'm not.

5. a. I'm studying in the library.
b. I study in the library.

13

cook	drive	play	skate	speak
dance	paint	sing	ski	use

1. Billy ____can't____ ____ski____.

   He ____can____ ____skate____.

2. Sally _____ _____.

   She _____ _____.

3. Edward _____ _____ pictures.

   He _____ _____ houses.

4. Carla _____ _____ Arabic.

   She _____ _____ Italian.

5. We _____ _____ Greek food.

   We _____ _____ Japanese food.

6. I _____ _____ a cash register.

   I _____ _____ a calculator.

7. They _____ _____ tennis.

   They _____ _____ baseball.

8. Harold _____ _____ a taxi.

   He _____ _____ a bus.

B WHAT CAN YOU DO?

Check the things you can do. Then ask other students.

Can you . . .?	You		Student 1		Student 2	
1. cook	❏ yes	❏ no	❏ yes	❏ no	❏ yes	❏ no
2. swim	❏ yes	❏ no	❏ yes	❏ no	❏ yes	❏ no
3. ski	❏ yes	❏ no	❏ yes	❏ no	❏ yes	❏ no
4. skate	❏ yes	❏ no	❏ yes	❏ no	❏ yes	❏ no
5. paint	❏ yes	❏ no	❏ yes	❏ no	❏ yes	❏ no
6. drive	❏ yes	❏ no	❏ yes	❏ no	❏ yes	❏ no
7. play tennis	❏ yes	❏ no	❏ yes	❏ no	❏ yes	❏ no
8. speak Chinese	❏ yes	❏ no	❏ yes	❏ no	❏ yes	❏ no
9. use a cash register	❏ yes	❏ no	❏ yes	❏ no	❏ yes	❏ no

C WHAT'S THE QUESTION?

1. _____Can he cook_____?
Yes, he can.

2. _____?
No, she can't.

3. _____?
Yes, they can.

4. _____?
Yes, I can.

5. _____?
No, he can't.

6. _____?
No, we can't.

D LISTENING

Listen and circle the word you hear.

1. (can)	can't	4. can	can't	7. can	can't	10. can	can't
2. can	can't	5. can	can't	8. can	can't	11. can	can't
3. can	can't	6. can	can't	9. can	can't	12. can	can't

E PUZZLE

actor	actress	baker	chef	dancer	mechanic	secretary	singer	teacher	truck driver

Across

4. She fixes cars every day.
6. He teaches in a school.
7. She acts in the movies.
9. He dances every day.
10. He acts on TV.

Down

1. She drives a truck.
2. He types every day.
3. He cooks in a restaurant.
5. He bakes pies and cakes.
8. She sings on TV.

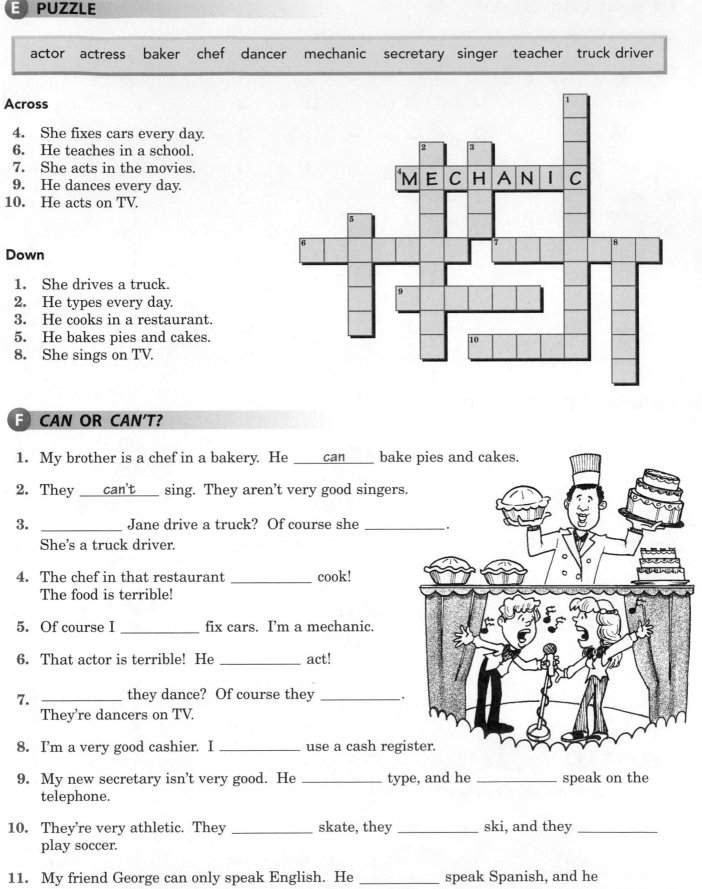

F CAN OR CAN'T?

1. My brother is a chef in a bakery. He ____can____ bake pies and cakes.

2. They ____can't____ sing. They aren't very good singers.

3. _____ Jane drive a truck? Of course she _____. She's a truck driver.

4. The chef in that restaurant _____ cook! The food is terrible!

5. Of course I _____ fix cars. I'm a mechanic.

6. That actor is terrible! He _____ act!

7. _____ they dance? Of course they _____. They're dancers on TV.

8. I'm a very good cashier. I _____ use a cash register.

9. My new secretary isn't very good. He _____ type, and he _____ speak on the telephone.

10. They're very athletic. They _____ skate, they _____ ski, and they _____ play soccer.

11. My friend George can only speak English. He _____ speak Spanish, and he _____ speak French.

Listen. Then clap and practice.

> She cán speak.
> He cán speak.
> We cán speak.
> They cán speak.

A. Can Anne speak French?

B. Of course she can.

She can speak French very well.

A. Can the Browns play tennis?

B. Of course they can.

They can play tennis very well.

A. Can Peter bake pies?

B. Of course he can.

He can bake pies very well.

A. Can we speak English?

B. Of course we can.

We can speak English very well.

have to	do	don't
has to	does	doesn't

1. Can you play baseball with me?

I'm sorry. I can't. I _have_ _to_ do my homework.

2. Why is Susie upset today?

She _____ _____ go to the dentist this afternoon.

3. Can your husband fix the sink?

No, he can't. He _____ _____ call a plumber.

4. Do I really _____ _____ get a haircut?

Yes, you do. You _____ _____ get a haircut today.

5. _____ Grandma _____ _____ go to the doctor often?

Yes, she _____. She _____ _____ go to the doctor every month.

6. _____ you _____ _____ work today?

No, I _____. I'm on vacation.

7. Do you want to go skiing this weekend?

This weekend? Sorry. We can't. We _____ _____ clean our apartment.

8. Are you bored?

No. I'm tired. I _____ _____ go to bed.

I A BUSY FAMILY

Mr. and Mrs. Lane, their son Danny, and their daughter Julie are very busy this week.

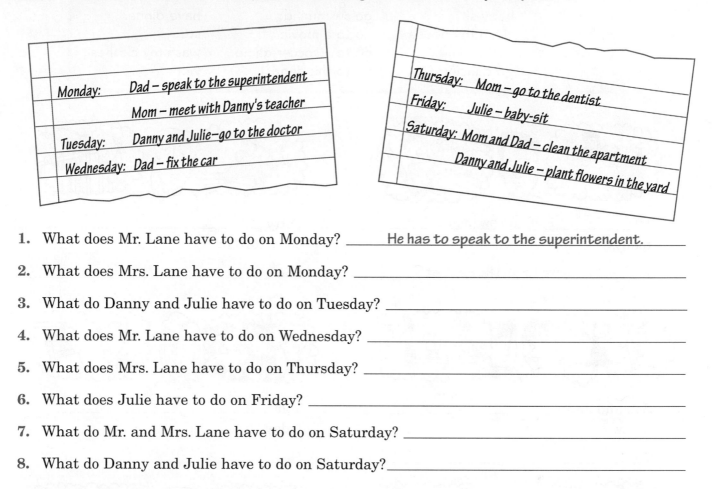

Monday: Dad – speak to the superintendent
           Mom – meet with Danny's teacher
Tuesday: Danny and Julie – go to the doctor
Wednesday: Dad – fix the car

Thursday: Mom – go to the dentist
Friday: Julie – baby-sit
Saturday: Mom and Dad – clean the apartment
           Danny and Julie – plant flowers in the yard

1. What does Mr. Lane have to do on Monday? _____ He has to speak to the superintendent. _____

2. What does Mrs. Lane have to do on Monday? _____

3. What do Danny and Julie have to do on Tuesday? _____

4. What does Mr. Lane have to do on Wednesday? _____

5. What does Mrs. Lane have to do on Thursday? _____

6. What does Julie have to do on Friday? _____

7. What do Mr. and Mrs. Lane have to do on Saturday? _____

8. What do Danny and Julie have to do on Saturday? _____

J WRITE ABOUT YOURSELF

What do YOU have to do this week?

....

....

....

....

K LISTENING

Listen and circle the words you hear.

1. has to   (have to)   4. has to   have to   7. can   can't

2. has to   have to   5. can   can't   8. has to   have to

3. can   can't   6. has to   have to   9. can   can't

can't	baby-sit	go swimming	have dinner
have to	clean the house	go to a movie	study
has to	go bowling	go to a soccer game	wash my clothes
	go dancing	go to the dentist	work

1. I _____ *can't go swimming* _____ today.

I _____ *have to go the dentist* _____ .

2. Patty _____ on Saturday.

She _____ .

3. Bob and Julie _____ today.

They _____ .

4. Tom _____ today.

He _____ .

5. We _____ on Saturday.

We _____ .

6. I _____ with you today.

I _____ .

M LISTENING

Listen and choose the correct answer.

1. a. She has to go to the dentist.
   b. She can go to the movies.

2. a. He has to wash his car.
   b. He can't go to the party.

3. a. She can have lunch with her friend.
   b. She can have dinner with her friend.

4. a. They have to paint their kitchen.
   b. They can go skiing.

5. a. He has to cook lunch.
   b. He has to go shopping today.

6. a. She has to baby-sit on Friday.
   b. She can't see a play on Saturday.

N **GRAMMARRAP:** *Where Is Everybody?*

Listen. Then clap and practice.

A. Where's Joe?

B. He has to go.

A. Where's Ray?

B. He can't stay.

A. Where's Kate?

B. She can't wait.

A. Where's Steve?

B. He has to leave.

A. Where's Murray?

B. He has to hurry.

A. What about you?

B. I have to go, too.

All. Oh, no!

Joe has to go.

Ray can't stay.

Kate can't wait.

Steve has to leave.

Murray has to hurry.

What can I do?

I have to go, too.

O **GRAMMARRAP:** *Can't Talk Now*

Listen. Then clap and practice.

A. I can't talk now.

I have to go to work.

B. I can't stop now.

I have to catch a train.

C. I can't leave now.

I have to make a call.

D. I can't stop now.

I have to catch a plane.

All. She can't stop now.

She has to catch a train.

She can't stop now.

She has to catch a plane.

A WHAT ARE THEY GOING TO DO?

1. What's Larry going to do tomorrow?

_____ He's going to cook. _____

2. What's Jane going to do tomorrow?

_____

3. What are you going to do tomorrow?

_____

4. What are they going to do tomorrow?

_____

5. What are you and your friends going to do tomorrow?

_____

6. What's William going to do tomorrow?

_____

B WHAT ARE THEY SAYING?

1. ____What are____ you

____going to do____ tomorrow?

____I'm going to____ clean my apartment.

2. _____ your husband

_____ tomorrow?

_____ fix the kitchen sink.

3. _____ your mother

_____ tomorrow?

_____ plant flowers.

4. _____ your cousins

_____ tomorrow?

_____ visit us.

C WHAT ARE THEY GOING TO DO?

are	is	going	go	to

1. We're ___going___ ___to___ ___go___ dancing tonight.

2. They're ___going___ swimming this afternoon.

3. I'm _____ _____ _____ shopping tomorrow.

4. Brian _____ _____ _____ the library this morning.

5. Rita _____ _____ _____ _____ _____ a party tomorrow night.

6. My friends and I _____ _____ to a baseball game tomorrow afternoon.

7. Mr. and Mrs. Lopez _____ _____ _____ _____ _____ a concert this evening.

8. I'm _____ _____ the supermarket tomorrow morning, and my husband

    _____ _____ _____ _____ _____ the bank.

D GRAMMARRAP: *What Are You Going to Do?*

Listen. Then clap and practice.

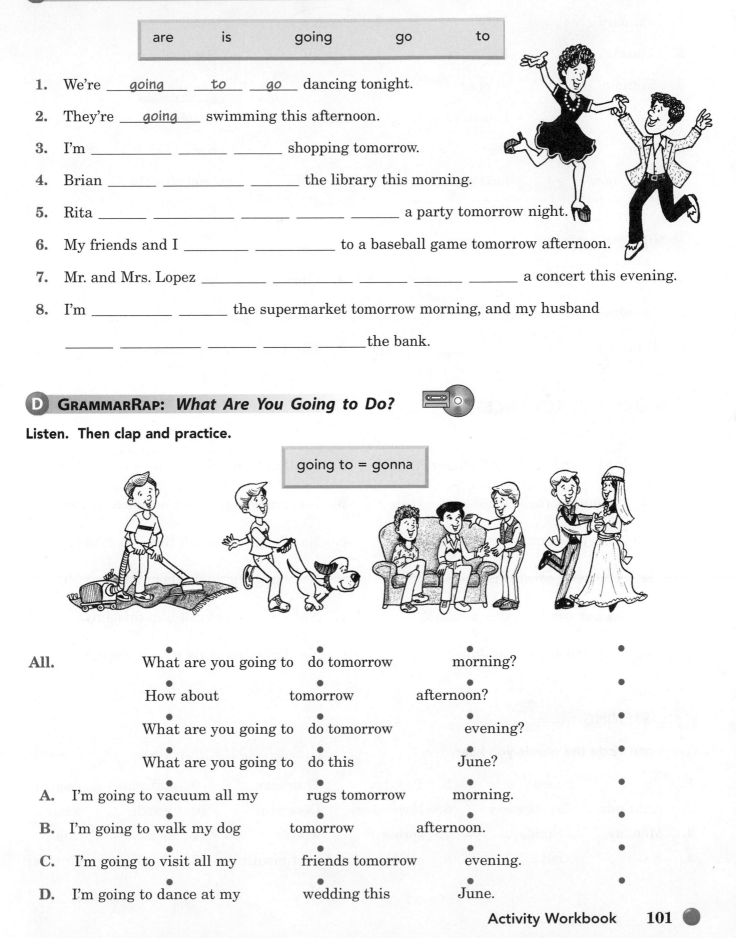

going to = gonna

All.   What are you going to   do tomorrow   morning?

How about   tomorrow   afternoon?

What are you going to   do tomorrow   evening?

What are you going to   do this   June?

A.   I'm going to vacuum all my   rugs tomorrow   morning.

B.   I'm going to walk my dog   tomorrow   afternoon.

C.   I'm going to visit all my   friends tomorrow   evening.

D.   I'm going to dance at my   wedding this   June.

Activity Workbook   **101**

E WHICH WORD DOESN'T BELONG?

1. January | May | (Monday) | April
2. Tuesday | Saturday | Sunday | September
3. autumn | at once | winter | summer
4. Friday | February | March | October
5. him | them | he | her
6. right now | next week | at once | immediately

F WHAT'S NEXT?

1. June   July   <u>August</u>
2. Monday   Tuesday   _____
3. February   March   _____

4. summer   fall   _____
5. Friday   Saturday   _____
6. October   November   _____

G MATCH THE SENTENCES

Are you going to . . .

<u>c</u> 1. call your friends on Thursday?

_____ 2. fix our doorbell this week?

_____ 3. visit your aunt next summer?

_____ 4. visit your cousins in April?

_____ 5. fix our windows this month?

_____ 6. call your uncle this June?

a. No. I'm going to visit them in October.

b. No. I'm going to visit her next winter.

c. No. I'm going to call them on Friday.

d. No. I'm going to fix them next month.

e. No. I'm going to call him this July.

f. No. I'm going to fix it next week.

H LISTENING

Listen and circle the words you hear.

1. (this) | next
2. right now | right away
3. Monday | Sunday
4. wash | cut
5. Tuesday | Thursday
6. November | December
7. spring | winter
8. at once | next month
9. autumn | August
10. watch | wash
11. next | this
12. number | plumber

1. We're going to <u>do our exercises</u> right now.   What _____ *are you going to do right now?* _____

2. She's going to baby-sit <u>this Friday</u>.   When _____

3. We're going to <u>Paris</u> next April.   Where _____

4. I'm going to clean it <u>because it's dirty</u>.   Why _____

5. They're going to <u>go to the beach</u> today.   What _____

6. I'm going to fix the doorbell <u>next week</u>.   When _____

7. She's going to plant flowers <u>in her yard</u>.   Where _____

8. He's going to read his e-mail <u>right now</u>.   When _____

9. I'm going to bed now <u>because I'm tired</u>.   Why _____

J **LISTENING**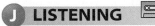

Listen to the following weather forecasts and circle the correct answers.

Today's Weather Forecast

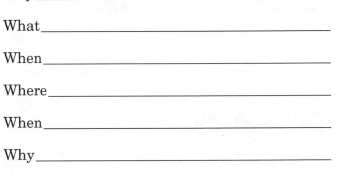

| **This afternoon:** | hot | (cool) | sunny | (cloudy) |
| **This evening:** | foggy | clear | rain | warm |

This Weekend's Weather Forecast

Tonight:	cool	cold	clear	warm
Saturday:	cloudy	sunny	foggy	hot
Sunday:	foggy	cool	snow	rain

Monday's Weather Forecast

Monday morning:	cold	cool	cloudy	nice
Monday afternoon:	cool	cold	foggy	snow
Tuesday morning:	sunny	cloudy	nice	warm

K WHAT DOES EVERYBODY WANT TO DO TOMORROW?

want to	wants to

1. I ___want to___ have a picnic tomorrow.

2. George _____ work in his garden.

3. Karen _____ take her children to a concert.

4. Mr. and Mrs. Sato _____ go to the beach.

5. You _____ see a movie.

6. I _____ see a play.

7. My friends _____ go to a basketball game.

L BAD WEATHER

| go skiing | go sailing | snow | be cold |
| take her son to the zoo | go jogging | rain | be warm |

1. What does Richard want to do tomorrow?

   _____He wants to go sailing._____

   What's the forecast?

   _____It's going to rain._____

2. What does Lucy want to do this afternoon?

   _____

   What's the forecast?

   _____

3. What do Carl and Betty want to do today?

   _____

   What's the forecast?

   _____

4. What does Jeff want to do tomorrow morning?

   _____

   What's the forecast?

   _____

YES AND NO

doesn't want to
don't want to

YES!   *NO!*

1. My parents want to buy a new car.   _They don't want to buy_ a motorcycle.

2. David wants to go to a baseball game.   _____ to a concert.

3. I want to wash my car.   _____ my clothes.

4. Nancy and Pam want to play baseball.   _____ soccer.

5. Michael wants to cook Italian food.   _____ American food.

6. We want to study English.   _____ history.

7. Margaret wants to dance with John.   _____ with Jim.

8. I want to work in the garden today.   _____ in the kitchen.

YES AND NO

I'm	not	
He She It	isn't	going to
We You They	aren't	

1. Steven is going to go swimming.   _He isn't going to go_ sailing.

2. I'm going to take a shower.   _____ a bath.

3. We're going to go bowling.   _____ shopping.

4. Barbara is going to go to the beach.   _____ to the mall.

5. My parents are going to clean the attic.   _____ the basement.

6. It's going to be warm.   _____ cool.

7. Robert is going to listen to the news.   _____ the forecast.

8. You're going to buy a used car.   _____ a new car.

WHAT DO THEY WANT TO BE?

Amy is an actress, but she wants to be a baker. She wants to work in a bakery and bake pies and cakes.

1. A. <u>What</u> <u>does</u> Amy <u>want</u> <u>to</u> be?

   B. _____ _____ _____ _____ a baker.

2. A. _____ _____ she _____ _____ work?

   B. _____ _____ _____ _____ in a bakery.

3. A. _____ _____ _____ _____ _____ bake?

   B. _____ _____ _____ _____ pies and cakes.

Marvin is a baker, but he wants to be an actor. He wants to sing and dance in movies in Hollywood.

4. A. _____ _____ Marvin _____ _____ be?

   B. _____ _____ _____ _____ an actor.

5. A. _____ _____ he _____ _____ work?

   B. _____ _____ _____ _____ in Hollywood.

6. A. _____ _____ _____ _____ _____ _____ do?

   B. _____ _____ _____ sing and dance.

P **WRITE ABOUT YOURSELF**

What do you want to be? What do you want to do? Where do you want to work?

....

....

....

....

....

Listen. Then clap and practice.

> want to = wanna
> wants to = wantsta

He wants to go.
I want to stay.
He wants to work.
I want to play.

She wants to eat at a restaurant.
I want to eat at home.
She wants to eat with all our friends.
I want to eat alone.

We want to leave at seven.
They want to leave at eight.
We want to get there early.
They want to get there late.

Jack wants to take the eight o'clock plane.
Joe wants to take the bus.
Bob wants to take the six o'clock train.
Bill wants to come with us.

Activity Workbook **107**

R WHAT TIME IS IT?

Draw the time on the clocks.

1. It's ten o'clock.

2. It's five fifteen.

3. It's nine thirty.

4. It's three forty-five.

5. It's noon.

6. It's half past eleven.

7. It's a quarter to one.

8. It's a quarter after two.

S WHICH TIMES ARE CORRECT?

Circle the correct times.

1. a. It's four o'clock.
   b. It's five o'clock. (circled)

2. a. It's eleven thirteen.
   b. It's eleven thirty.

3. a. It's a quarter after nine.
   b. It's three fifteen.

4. a. It's noon.
   b. It's midnight.

5. a. It's half past six.
   b. It's twelve thirty.

6. a. It's two fifteen.
   b. It's a quarter to three.

7. a. It's one thirty.
   b. It's one forty-five.

8. a. It's a quarter to seven.
   b. It's a quarter after seven.

9. a. It's six o'clock.
   b. It's midnight.

T LISTENING

Listen and write the time you hear.

1. ___7:45___

2. _____

3. _____

4. _____

5. _____

6. _____

7. _____

8. _____

9. _____

10. _____

11. _____

12. _____

U ALAN CHANG'S DAY

Alan Chang gets up every day at seven fifteen. He brushes his teeth and takes a shower. At seven forty-five he eats breakfast and reads his e-mail. At eight thirty he leaves the house and drives to work. Alan works at a computer company. He begins work at nine o'clock. Every day he uses business software on the computer and talks to people on the telephone. At twelve o'clock Adam is always hungry and thirsty. He eats lunch in the cafeteria. Alan leaves work at five thirty. He eats dinner at six o'clock and then at half past seven he watches videos on his new DVD player.

1. What time does Alan get up every day?   *He gets up at 7:15.*

2. What time does he eat breakfast?   _____

3. What time does he leave the house?   _____

4. What time does he begin work?   _____

5. Where does Alan work?   _____

6. What does he do at noon?   _____

7. What does he do at half past five?   _____

8. What time does he eat dinner?   _____

9. What does he do at seven thirty?   _____

V YOUR DAY

Answer in complete sentences.

1. What time do you usually get up?   ....

2. What do you do after you get up?   ....

3. When do you usually leave for school or work?   ....

4. What time do you usually have lunch?   ....

5. When do you get home from school or work?   ....

6. What time do you usually have dinner?   ....

7. What do you usually do after dinner?   ....

8. When do you usually go to bed?   ....

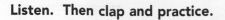
Listen. Then clap and practice.

Time flies.

The days go by.

Monday, Tuesday,

Wednesday, Thursday,

Friday, Saturday.

Time flies.

The days go by.

Time flies.

The months go by.

January, February, March, April,

May, June, July, August,

September, October, November, December.

Time flies.

The months go by.

The seasons come,

The seasons go.

Autumn, winter, spring, summer,

Autumn, winter, spring, summer.

Time flies.

The years go by.

Where do they go?

I don't know.

I'm	going	be	after	day	year	December	April	right
it's	wait	in	past	month	fall	February	July	
you	waiting	to	with	week	summer	September		

Any day, any ___week___ 1, any month, any _____ 2, I'm _____ _____ 3

wait right here to be with you.

_____ 4 the spring, in the _____ 5, in the winter, or the _____ 6, just call.

I'm _____ 7 here to be with you.

_____ _____ 8 to wait from January, _____ 9 March,

_____ 10, May, June and _____ 11, August, _____ 12, October,

and November, and all of _____ 13. I'm going to wait . . .

_____ 14 one o'clock, a quarter _____ 15. It's half _____ 16 one, a quarter

_____ 17 two. And I'm going _____ _____ 18 right here to be with you.

Any _____ 19, any week, any _____ 20, any year, I'm going to wait

_____ 21 here to be _____ 22 you.

Yes, I'm going to wait right here _____ _____ 23 with _____ 24.

A.

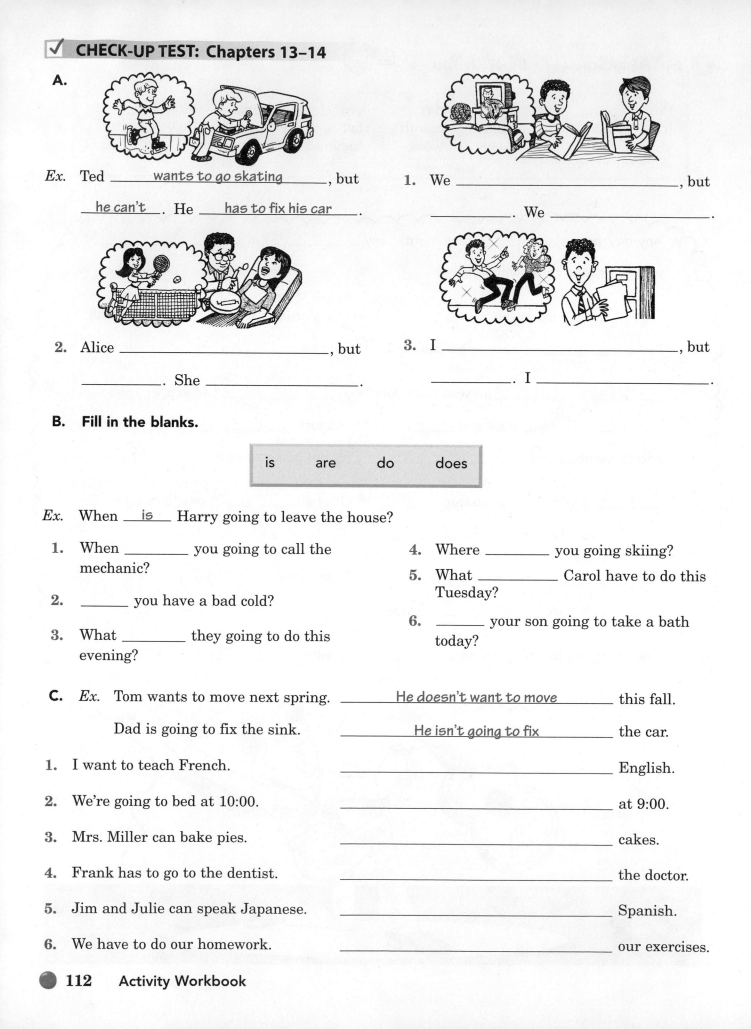

Ex. Ted _____wants to go skating_____, but _____he can't_____. He _____has to fix his car_____.

1. We _____, but _____. We _____.

2. Alice _____, but _____. She _____.

3. I _____, but _____. I _____.

B. Fill in the blanks.

is	are	do	does

Ex. When ___is___ Harry going to leave the house?

1. When _____ you going to call the mechanic?

2. _____ you have a bad cold?

3. What _____ they going to do this evening?

4. Where _____ you going skiing?

5. What _____ Carol have to do this Tuesday?

6. _____ your son going to take a bath today?

C. *Ex.* Tom wants to move next spring. _____He doesn't want to move_____ this fall.

Dad is going to fix the sink. _____He isn't going to fix_____ the car.

1. I want to teach French. _____ English.

2. We're going to bed at 10:00. _____ at 9:00.

3. Mrs. Miller can bake pies. _____ cakes.

4. Frank has to go to the dentist. _____ the doctor.

5. Jim and Julie can speak Japanese. _____ Spanish.

6. We have to do our homework. _____ our exercises.

D. Every day Helen gets up at 7:30. At 8:00 she eats breakfast, and at 8:30 she goes to work. At noon she has lunch, and at 5:00 she takes the bus home. What's Helen going to do tomorrow?

Tomorrow Helen _____*is going to get up*_____ at 7:30. At 8:00 she's

_____¹ breakfast, and at 8:30 _____² to work. At noon

_____³ lunch, and at 5:00 _____⁴ home.

E. Write the question.

What	When	Where

Ex. I'm going to clean my house <u>this evening</u>.   <u>When are you going to clean your house?</u>

1. She's going to <u>fix her sink</u> tomorrow.   _____

2. He's going to play tennis <u>in the park</u>.   _____

3. I'm going to go to the zoo <u>this weekend</u>.   _____

4. They're going to study <u>Spanish</u> next year.   _____

F. What time is it?

Ex.

It's ten o'clock.

1.

It's five fifteen.

2.

It's nine thirty.

3.

It's noon.

4.

It's two forty-five.

5.

It's a quarter after eleven.

G. Listen to the story. Fill in the correct times.

English	_____	Chinese	_____	lunch	_____
mathematics	_____	science	_____	music	_____

A WHAT'S THE MATTER?

| backache | cough | fever | sore throat | toothache |
| cold | earache | headache | stomachache | |

1. He _____has a cold_____ _____.

2. She _____ _____.

3. I _____ _____.

4. She _____ _____.

5. I _____ _____.

6. He _____ _____.

7. She _____ _____.

8. You _____ _____.

9. He _____ _____.

B LISTENING

Listen to the story. Put the number under the correct picture.

_____   1   _____   _____

_____   _____   _____   _____

C GRAMMARRAP: *What's the Matter?*

Listen. Then clap and practice.

A. What's the matter with   you?

B.   I have a headache.

     What's the matter with   YOU?

A.   I have a cold.

A. What's the matter with   him?

B.   He has a toothache.

     What's the matter with   HER?

A.   She has a cold.

A. What's the matter with   Mary?

B.   She has an earache.

     What's the matter with   BILL?

A.   He has a very bad   cold.

A. What's the matter with   Fred?

B.   He has a backache.

     What's the matter with   ANNE?

A. She has an awful   cold.

A. What's the matter with   Jane?

B.   She has a stomachache.

     What's the matter with   PAUL?

A.   He has a terrible   cold.

A. What's the matter with the   students?

B.   They have sore   throats.

     What's the matter with the   teachers?

A.   They have terrible   colds.

     They have terrible   terrible

     colds!

bake	cook	dance	rest	shout	study
clean	cry	paint	shave	smile	type

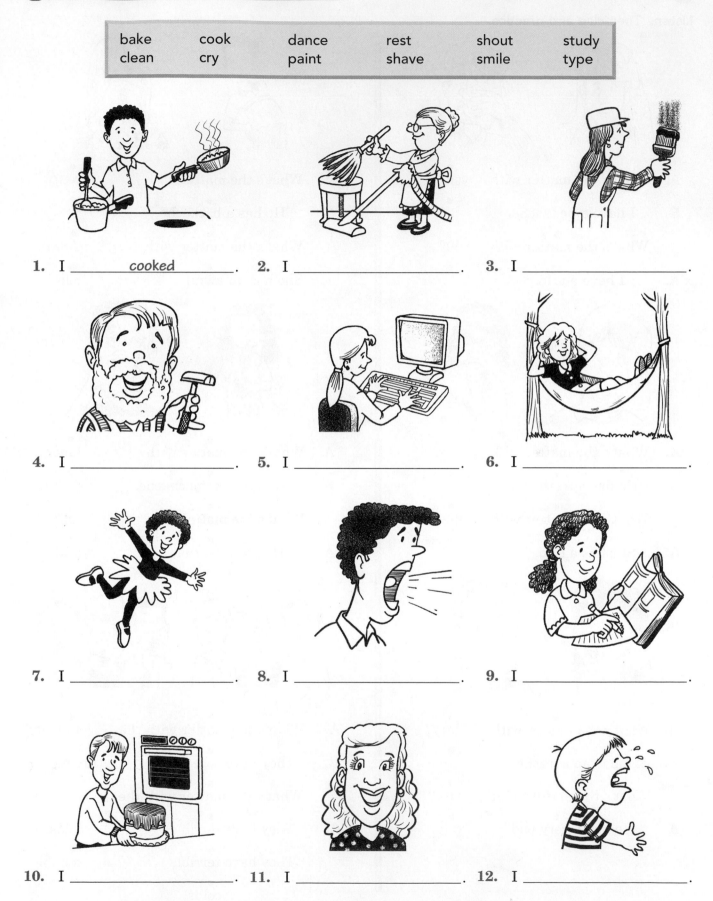

1. I _____ cooked _____ .

2. I _____ .

3. I _____ .

4. I _____ .

5. I _____ .

6. I _____ .

7. I _____ .

8. I _____ .

9. I _____ .

10. I _____ .

11. I _____ .

12. I _____ .

WHAT'S THE WORD?

| brush | cook | paint | plant | play | study | wait | watch | work |

1. I _____work_____ in an office every day.

2. I _____played_____ the guitar yesterday.

3. I _____ my teeth every day.

4. I _____ flowers yesterday.

5. I _____ dinner every day.

6. I _____ English yesterday.

7. I _____ my fence yesterday.

8. I _____ TV every day.

9. I _____ for the bus yesterday.

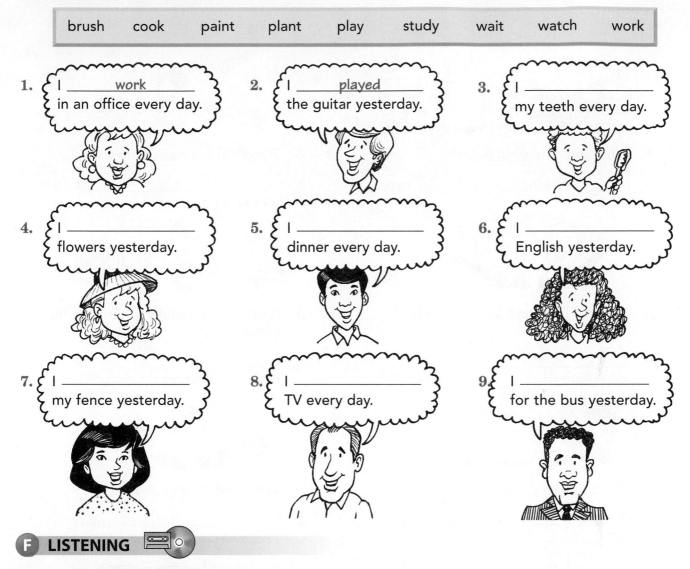

F **LISTENING** 💿

Listen and circle the correct answer.

Ex. I study.   yesterday
(every day)

I played cards.   (yesterday)
every day

1. yesterday
every day

2. yesterday
every day

3. yesterday
every day

4. yesterday
every day

5. yesterday
every day

6. yesterday
every day

7. yesterday
every day

8. yesterday
every day

9. yesterday
every day

10. yesterday
every day

11. yesterday
every day

12. yesterday
every day

Activity Workbook 117

bark	clean	cry	drink	eat	ride	sing	sit	skate	write

1. A. What did James do today?

   B. _____He cleaned_____ his apartment all day.

2. A. What did your sister do today?

   B. _____ letters all morning.

3. A. What did Mr. and Mrs. Porter do yesterday?

   B. _____ songs all evening.

4. A. What did you and your friends do today?

   B. _____ in the park all afternoon.

5. A. What did Linda do yesterday?

   B. _____ lemonade all morning.

6. A. What did Jimmy do today?

   B. _____ candy and cookies all day.

7. A. What did Mrs. Mason's children do today?

   B. _____ all afternoon.

8. A. What did the neighbors' dogs do yesterday?

   B. _____ all night.

9. A. What did Howard do yesterday?

   B. _____ in the clinic all evening.

10. A. What did Grandma do today?

    B. _____ her bicycle all afternoon.

H PUZZLE

Across

3. ride
4. study
6. eat

Down

1. cry
2. work
4. sit
5. drink

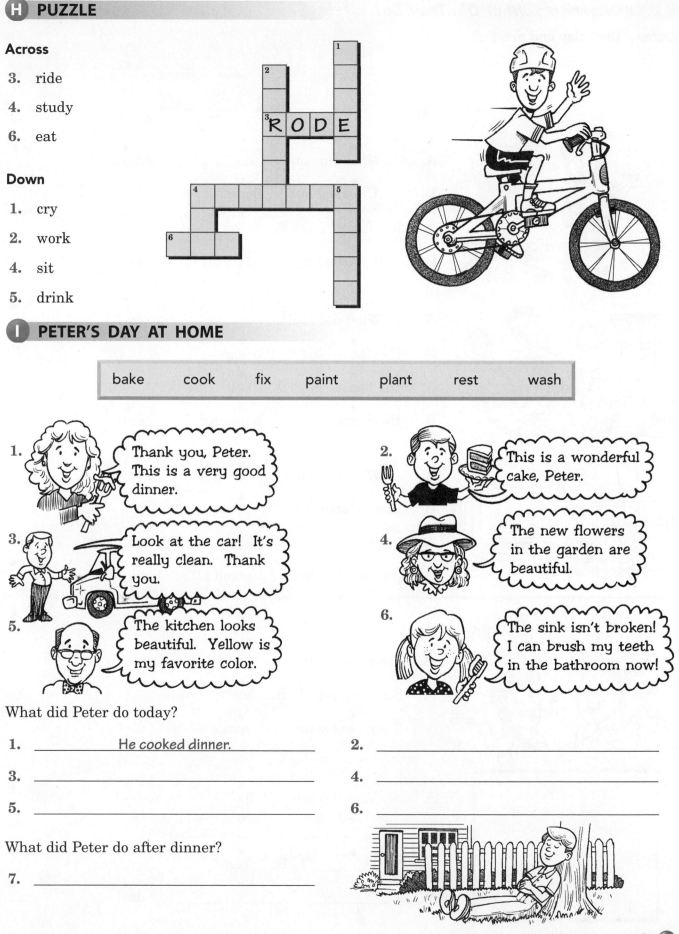

Crossword: 3 Across — R O D E

I PETER'S DAY AT HOME

| bake | cook | fix | paint | plant | rest | wash |

1. Thank you, Peter. This is a very good dinner.

2. This is a wonderful cake, Peter.

3. Look at the car! It's really clean. Thank you.

4. The new flowers in the garden are beautiful.

5. The kitchen looks beautiful. Yellow is my favorite color.

6. The sink isn't broken! I can brush my teeth in the bathroom now!

What did Peter do today?

1. _____He cooked dinner._____   2. _____

3. _____   4. _____

5. _____   6. _____

What did Peter do after dinner?

7. _____

Activity Workbook   **119**

J **GRAMMARRAP:** *What Did They Do?*

Listen. Then clap and practice.

washed [t]	cleaned [d]	painted [ɪd]

A. What did you   do   today?

B.   I washed my   floors.

A. Your floors?   **B.**   Yes!

B.   I washed my   floors all   day!

A.   What did Mark   do   today?

B. He cleaned his   house.

A. His house?   **B.**   Yes!

B. He cleaned his   house all   day!

A.   What did Pam   do   today?

B. She painted her   porch.

A.   Her porch?   **B.**   Yes!

B. She painted her   porch all   day!

A.   What did they   do   today?

B. They sang some   songs.

A. Some songs?   **B.**   Yes!

They sang some   songs all   day!

A.   What did you   do   today?

B. I _____.

A. _____? **B.**   Yes!

B. I _____ all day!

At my grandfather's birthday party last night, everybody (listen) _____listened_____ ¹ to Mexican music and (dance) _____². My sister Gloria (sing) _____³ my grandfather's favorite songs all evening, and my brother Daniel (play) _____⁴ the guitar.

Everybody (sit) _____⁵ in the living room with my grandmother and grandfather and (look) _____⁶ at old photographs. We (laugh) _____⁷, we (smile) _____⁸, we (cry) _____⁹, and we (talk) _____¹⁰about "the good old days." What did I do at my grandfather's birthday party? I (drink) _____¹¹ lemonade and (eat) _____¹² a lot of food!

L **MATCHING**

___e___ **1.** At the party my brother played _____.

_____ **2.** Everybody sat and talked about _____.

_____ **3.** My sister has a sore throat today because _____.

_____ **4.** We all looked at _____.

_____ **5.** We listened to _____.

_____ **6.** I have a toothache today because I _____.

_____ **7.** I also have a stomachache because I _____.

a. drank lemonade all night

b. Mexican music

c. "the good old days"

d. ate a lot of food

e. the guitar

f. old photographs

g. she sang all evening

1. Jennifer brushed her teeth last night.

    She didn't brush her teeth.

    She brushed her hair.

2. Kevin played the violin yesterday afternoon.

    _____

    _____

3. Harold and Betty listened to the news yesterday evening.

    _____

    _____

4. Mrs. Martinez waited for the train this afternoon.

    _____

    _____

5. Frank fixed his fence yesterday morning.

    _____

    _____

6. Mr. and Mrs. Park cleaned their attic today.

    _____

    _____

7. Marvin baked a pie yesterday evening.

    _____

    _____

8. Patty called her grandmother last night.

    _____

    _____

B ALAN AND HIS SISTER

Alan and his sister Ellen did very different things yesterday. Alan (rest) _____rested_____¹ all day. He didn't (work) _____², and he didn't (study) _____³. He (listen) _____⁴ to music yesterday morning. He (watch) _____⁵ game shows on TV yesterday afternoon. And yesterday evening he (talk) _____⁶ to his friends on the telephone and (play) _____⁷ games on his computer.

Ellen didn't (listen) _____⁸ to music. She didn't (watch) _____⁹ game shows on TV, and she didn't (play) _____¹⁰ games on her computer   What did she do? She (study) _____¹¹ English yesterday morning. She (clean) _____¹² the yard yesterday afternoon. And she (cook) _____¹³ dinner for her family last night.

C YES AND NO

1. Did Alan rest all day yesterday?   _____Yes, he did._____

2. Did Ellen rest all day yesterday?   _____No, she didn't._____

3. Did Ellen study yesterday morning?   _____

4. Did Alan study yesterday morning?   _____

5. Did Alan watch TV yesterday afternoon?   _____

6. _____Did Ellen clean_____ the yard yesterday afternoon?   Yes, she did.

7. _____ to his friends yesterday evening?   Yes, he did.

8. _____ dinner for his family last night?   No, he didn't.

9. _____ to music yesterday morning?   No, she didn't.

10. _____ game shows yesterday afternoon?   No, she didn't.

11. _____ English yesterday afternoon?   No, he didn't.

D WHAT DID THEY DO?

1. I didn't buy a car. I ____bought____ a motorcycle.

2. Michael didn't have a headache. He _____ a toothache.

3. Alice didn't write to her uncle. She _____ to her cousin.

4. We didn't do our homework last night. We _____ yoga.

5. They didn't take the bus to work today. They _____ the train.

6. Barbara didn't get up at 7:00 this morning. She _____ up at 6:00.

7. My friend and I didn't go swimming yesterday. We _____ bowling.

8. Martha didn't read the newspaper last night. She _____ a book.

9. My children didn't make breakfast this morning. They _____ lunch.

E THEY DIDN'T DO WHAT THEY USUALLY DO

1. Robert usually writes to his friends.
   He ___didn't___ ___write___ to his friends yesterday.
   He ___wrote___ to his grandparents.

2. I usually have a cold in January.
   I _____ _____ a cold last January.
   I _____ a cold last July.

3. We usually eat at home on Friday night.
   We _____ _____ at home last Friday night.
   We _____ at a very nice restaurant.

4. Bill usually gets up 7:00 o'clock.
   He _____ _____ up at 7:00 this morning.
   He _____ up at 10:00.

5. Tom and Tina usually go dancing every week.
   They _____ _____ dancing this week.
   They _____ sailing.

6. Susie usually drinks milk every afternoon.
   She _____ _____ milk this afternoon.
   She _____ lemonade.

7. My brother usually makes lunch on Sunday.
   He _____ _____ lunch last Sunday.
   He _____ dinner.

8. Mr. Lee usually takes his wife to the movies.
   He _____ _____ his wife to the movies last night.
   He _____ his daughter and his son-in-law.

9. We usually buy food at a large supermarket.
   We _____ _____ food at a supermarket today.
   We _____ food at a small grocery store.

10. I usually sit next to Maria in English class.
    I _____ _____ next to Maria yesterday.
    I _____ next to her sister Carmen.

A.   Did she wash her   skirt?

B.   No, she   didn't.

A.   What did she   wash?

B.   She washed her   __shirt__ .

A.   Did they paint the   door?

B.   No, they   didn't.

A.   What did they paint?

B.   They painted the   _____ .

A.   Did he call his   mother?

B.   No, he   didn't.

A.   Who did he   call?

B.   He called his   _____ .

A.   Did you buy   new suits?

B.   No, we   didn't.

A.   What did you   buy?

B.   We bought new   _____ .

A.   Did you get up at   seven?

B.   No, I   didn't.

A.   When did you get   up?

B.   I got up at   _____ .

WHAT'S THE ANSWER?

1. Did Henry ride his bicycle to work this morning?   Yes, ___*he did*___ .

2. Did you get up at 6:00 this morning?   No, _____ .

3. Did your sister call you last night?   Yes, _____ .

4. Did Mr. and Mrs. Chen clean their apartment last weekend?   No, _____ .

5. Did you and your friends go to the library yesterday afternoon?   Yes, _____ .

6. Did your father make spaghetti for dinner last night?   No, _____ .

7. Excuse me. Did I take your gloves?   Yes, _____ .

8. Bob, did you do your exercises today?   No, _____ .

H **WHAT'S THE QUESTION?**

1. ___*Did she buy*___ a car?   No, she didn't. She bought a truck.

2. _____ a headache?   No, he didn't. He had a backache.

3. _____ a shower?   No, I didn't. I took a bath.

4. _____ to the supermarket?   No, they didn't. They went to the bank.

5. _____ in the living room?   No, we didn't. We sat in the kitchen.

6. _____ a right turn?   No, you didn't. You made a left turn.

I **LISTENING**

Listen and choose the correct response.

1. a. I write to her every day.
   b. I wrote to her this morning. *(circled)*

2. a. He washes it every weekend.
   b. He washed it last weekend.

3. a. They visit my aunt and my uncle.
   b. They visited my aunt and my uncle.

4. a. She did yoga in the park.
   b. She does yoga in the park.

5. a. He went to sleep at 8:00.
   b. He goes to sleep at 8:00.

6. a. We clean it every weekend.
   b. We cleaned it last weekend.

7. a. We take them to the zoo.
   b. We took them to the zoo.

8. a. I make spaghetti.
   b. I made spaghetti.

9. a. She reads it every afternoon.
   b. She read it this afternoon.

10. a. I get up at 7:00.
    b. I got up at 7:00.

forget	go	have to	miss
get up	have	meet	steal

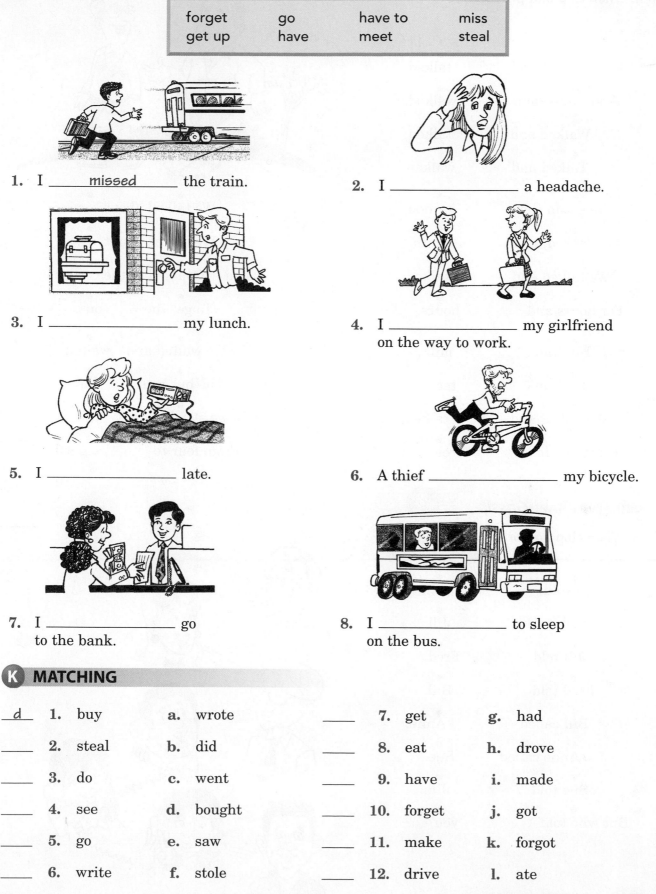

1. I _____missed_____ the train.

2. I _____ a headache.

3. I _____ my lunch.

4. I _____ my girlfriend on the way to work.

5. I _____ late.

6. A thief _____ my bicycle.

7. I _____ go to the bank.

8. I _____ to sleep on the bus.

K MATCHING

_d_	1. buy	a. wrote		___	7. get	g. had
___	2. steal	b. did		___	8. eat	h. drove
___	3. do	c. went		___	9. have	i. made
___	4. see	d. bought		___	10. forget	j. got
___	5. go	e. saw		___	11. make	k. forgot
___	6. write	f. stole		___	12. drive	l. ate

GRAMMARRAP: *Old Friends*

Listen. Then clap and practice.

We walked and   talked

And talked and   walked.

Walked and   talked,

Talked and   walked.

We sat in the   garden

And looked at the   flowers.

We talked and   talked

For hours and   hours.

He drank   milk,

And I drank   tea.

We talked and   talked

From one to   three.

We talked about him.

We talked about us.

Then we walked to the corner

To get the   bus.

We waited and   waited.

The bus was   late.

So we stood and   talked

From four to   eight.

M **GRAMMARRAP:** *Gossip*

Listen. Then clap and practice.

I told   Jack.

Jack told   Jill.

Jill told   Fred.

Fred told   Bill.

Bill called   Anne.

Anne called   Sue.

Sue told   Jim.

But who told   you?

was   were

We ____were____¹ very upset at work last Friday. Our computers _____² broken, our boss _____³ angry because he _____⁴ tired, and my friends and I _____⁵ sick. Outside it _____⁶ cloudy and it _____⁷ very cold. And then in the afternoon all the trains _____⁸ late. I _____⁹ hungry when I got home, and my children _____¹⁰ very noisy. It _____¹¹ a terrible day!

We ____were____¹² very happy at work on Monday. Our computers _____¹³ fine, our boss _____¹⁴ happy, and my friends and I _____¹⁵ energetic. Outside it _____¹⁶ sunny, it _____¹⁷ warm, and all the trains _____¹⁸ early. My children _____¹⁹ very quiet when I got home. We ate a big dinner, and I _____²⁰ very full. It was a wonderful day!

B LISTENING

Listen and circle the word you hear.

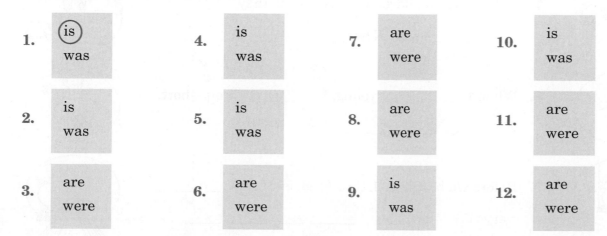

1. (is)
   was

2. is
   was

3. are
   were

4. is
   was

5. is
   was

6. are
   were

7. are
   were

8. are
   were

9. is
   was

10. is
    was

11. are
    were

12. are
    were

| clean | enormous | happy | shiny | thin |
| comfortable | full | healthy | tall | |

1. Before I took A-1 Vitamins, I ___was___ always

   sick. Now __I'm__ ___healthy___.

2. Before Harold met Gertrude, he _____ sad.

   Now _____ _____ all the time.

3. Before we ate a big breakfast today, we _____

   hungry. Now _____ _____.

4. Before Helen got her new sofa, she _____

   uncomfortable. Now _____ very _____.

5. Before you drank A-1 Skim Milk, you _____

   heavy. Now _____ _____.

6. Before Charlie used A-1 Car Wax, his car _____

   dull. Now _____ _____.

7. Before these children used A-1 soap, they

   _____ dirty. Now _____ _____.

8. When I _____ young, I _____ very short.

   Now _____ _____.

9. Before we bought A-1 Bird Food, our birds _____

   very tiny. Now _____ _____.

WHAT'S THE WORD?

1. A. ____Were____ you at a concert last night?

   B. No, I ___wasn't___. I ___was___ at a play.

2. A. _____ your neighbors quiet last Saturday night?

   B. No, they _____. They _____ very noisy.

3. A. _____ your boss in the office yesterday?

   B. No, she _____. She _____ on vacation.

4. A. _____ we at home last Tuesday?

   B. No, we _____. We _____ at the mall.

5. A. _____ the questions on the examination easy?

   B. No, they _____. They _____ very difficult.

6. A. _____ Timothy on time for his wedding?

   B. No, he _____. He _____ late.

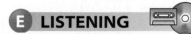

E **LISTENING**

Listen and circle the word you hear.

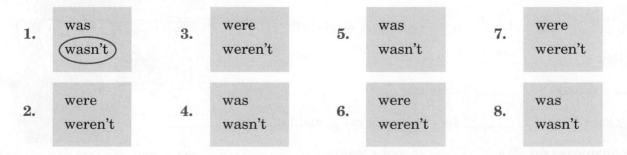

1. was / (wasn't)
2. were / weren't
3. were / weren't
4. was / wasn't
5. was / wasn't
6. were / weren't
7. were / weren't
8. was / wasn't

F WHAT'S THE WORD?

did	was	were
didn't	wasn't	weren't

A. Why _____did_____ ¹ Victor leave the party early?

B. He _____ ² like the party. It _____ ³ noisy, the food
_____ ⁴ very good, and his friends _____ ⁵ there.

A. Where _____ ⁶ you last week? You _____ ⁷ at work.

B. That's right. I _____ ⁸.

A. _____ ⁹ you sick?

B. Yes, I _____ ¹⁰. I _____ ¹¹ very sick. I had an earache and a cold.

A. _____ ¹² you also have a headache?

B. No. I _____ ¹³ have a headache, but I had a sore throat.

I _____ ¹⁴ go to work all week. I _____ ¹⁵ really sick!

A. How _____ ¹⁶ your vacation?

B. It _____ ¹⁷ terrible!

A. That's too bad. _____ ¹⁸ you like the hotel?

B. No, we _____ ¹⁹. The bathroom sink _____ ²⁰ broken,

the hotel room _____ ²¹ clean, and we _____ ²² sleep well

at night because the people in the next room _____ ²³ very loud.

A. _____ ²⁴ you swim at the beach?

B. No, we _____ ²⁵. The weather _____ ²⁶ very cold!

A. _____ ²⁷ your grandchildren visit you last weekend?

B. No, they _____ ²⁸.

A. That's too bad. _____ ²⁹ they busy?

B. My grandson _____ ³⁰ feel well, and my granddaughter _____ ³¹

on a business trip. We _____ ³² sad because we _____ ³³ see them.

G GRAMMARRAP: *Were You Late This Morning?*

Listen. Then clap and practice.

A.   Were you late this   morning?

B.   No, I wasn't. I was   early.

A.   Was he sick last   night?

B.   No, he wasn't. He was   fine.

A.   Was her hair very   straight?

B.   No, it wasn't. It was   curly.

A. Were there eight new   lessons?

B. No, there weren't. There were   nine.

A.   Was the movie   short?

B.   No, it wasn't. It was   long.

A.   Was the food   expensive?

B.   No, it wasn't. It was   free.

A.   Was I right?

B.   No, you weren't. You were   wrong.

A.   Were the tickets two   dollars?

B.   No, they weren't.   They were three.

basketball	did	freckles	short	subjects	wasn't	weren't
curly	didn't	hobby	sports	was	were	

A. Tell me, what ___ _did_ ¹ you look like when you _____² young? _____³ you tall?

B. No, I _____⁴. I _____⁵ _____⁶.

A. _____⁷ you have straight hair?

B. No, I _____⁸. I had _____⁹ hair.

A. Oh. And _____¹⁰ you have dimples?

B. No, I _____¹¹, but I had _____¹².

A. I'm sure you _____¹³ very cute!

What _____¹⁴ you do with your friends?

B. We played sports.

A. Oh. What _____¹⁵ you play?

B. We played _____¹⁶ and tennis.

A. Tell me, _____¹⁷ you like school?

B. Yes. I liked school a lot.

A. What _____¹⁸ your favorite _____¹⁹?

B. English and mathematics.

A. _____²⁰ you have a _____²¹?

B. Yes, I _____²². I played chess.

I **LISTENING**

Listen and choose the correct response.

1.   a. I was born last week.
   ⓑ I was born in Japan.

2.   a. Yes, I did.
   b. I grew up in Tokyo.

3.   a. English.
   b. No, I didn't.

4.   a. In Los Angeles.
   b. Last year.

5.   a. I was tall and thin.
   b. I didn't look.

6.   a. No. I had straight hair.
   b. No. I had dimples.

7.   a. I played sports.
   b. I play chess.

8.   a. Yes. I'm here.
   b. Yes. My father.

Listen. Then clap and practice.

A. The teacher was   there,

But where were the   students?

B. The students were   there.

All.   Where?

A. The teacher was   there,

The students were   there,

But where were the   books?

B. The books were   there.

All.   Where?

A. The teacher was   there,

The students were   there,

The books were   there,

But where was the   chalk?

B. The chalk was   there.

All.   Where?

A. The teacher was   there,

The students were   there,

The books were   there,

The chalk was   there,

But where were the   chairs?

B. The chairs were   there.

All.   Where?

B.   There.

All.   Where?

B. Right there!

Right   there!

A. Fill in the blanks.

was	were	wasn't	weren't

1. A. ____Was____ Barbara at work yesterday?

    B. No, she _____. She _____ sick.

2. A. Why _____ you late today?

    B. I _____ late because I _____ on time for the bus.

3. A. Where _____ Grandma and Grandpa last night? They _____ at home.

    B. They _____ at a concert.

B. Complete the sentences.

Ex. Before we washed our car, it ____was____ dirty. Now ____it's____ ____clean____.

1. Before I ate dinner, I _____ hungry. Now _____ _____.

2. When I got my cats, they _____ tiny. Now _____ _____.

3. When we _____ in college, we _____ thin. Now _____ _____.

4. When I was young, I _____ energetic. Now _____ _____.

C. Complete the sentences.

Ex. a. Carla usually studies English. She ____didn't____ ____study____ English yesterday. She ____studied____ mathematics.

b. Paul usually writes to his friends. He ____didn't____ ____write____ to his friends yesterday. He ____wrote____ to his cousins.

1. I usually drive to the park on Saturday. I _____ _____ to the park last Saturday. I _____ to the mall.

2. We usually arrive late. We _____ _____ late today. We _____ on time.

3. My husband and my son usually shave in the morning. They _____ _____ in the morning today. They _____ in the afternoon.

4. Bob usually goes jogging in the evening. He _____ _____ jogging yesterday evening. He _____ dancing.

5. Margaret usually reads the newspaper in the morning. She _____ _____ the newspaper yesterday morning. She _____ a magazine.

D. Write the question.

Ex. _____Did they get up_____ at 8:00?   No, they didn't. They got up at 10:00.

1. _____ his brother?   No, he didn't. He met his sister.

2. _____ her bicycle?   No, she didn't. She rode her motorcycle.

3. _____ a good time?   No, we didn't. We had a terrible time.

4. _____ lunch?   No, they didn't. They made dinner.

5. _____ a movie?   No, I didn't. I saw a play.

E. Read the story and then write about yesterday.

Every morning I get up early. I brush my teeth, and I do my exercises. Then I sit in the kitchen and I eat breakfast. At 8:00 I go to work. I walk to the drug store and I buy a newspaper. Then I take the train to my office. I don't take the bus, and I don't drive my car.

Yesterday I ____got up____ early. I _____ ¹ my teeth, and I _____ ²

my exercises. Then I _____ ³ in the kitchen and I _____ ⁴ breakfast. At 8:00 I

_____ ⁵ to work. I _____ ⁶ to the drug store and I _____ ⁷ a

newspaper. Then I _____ ⁸ the train to my office. I _____ _____ ⁹

the bus, and I _____ _____ ¹⁰ my car.

F. Listen and circle the word you hear.

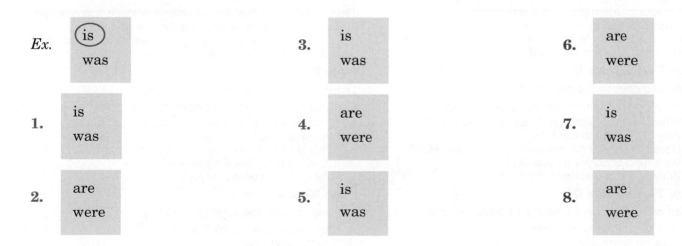

Ex.   (is)
        was

1.   is
     was

2.   are
     were

3.   is
     was

4.   are
     were

5.   is
     was

6.   are
     were

7.   is
     was

8.   are
     were

Listening Scripts

Page 63 Exercise B

Listen and choose the correct response.

1. What's your name?
2. What language do you speak?
3. What do they do every day?
4. Where do you live?
5. What language do you speak?
6. What do you do every day?

Page 66 Exercise G

Listen and circle the word you hear.

1. We live in Paris.
2. Where do you live?
3. What language does he speak?
4. Every day I listen to Greek music.
5. Every day she watches English TV shows.
6. What do they eat every day?
7. Every day I sing Korean songs.
8. Every day she eats Chinese food.
9. Every day he reads Mexican newspapers.

Page 70 Exercise D

Listen and choose the correct response.

1. What kind of food do you like?
2. Do they paint houses?
3. Why does he go to that restaurant?
4. When does Mrs. Miller cook dinner?
5. Do you work in a bank?
6. Where do they live?
7. What do your children do in the park?
8. Does your friend Patty drive a taxi?
9. Why do they shop in that store?

Page 72 Exercise I

Listen and choose the correct response.

1. Do you do a different kind of sport every day?
2. Does Bob write for the school newspaper?
3. Do Mr. and Mrs. Chang live near a bus stop?
4. Does your sister baby-sit every weekend?
5. Does Timmy do a different activity every day?
6. Do your children play in the orchestra?
7. Does your son sing in the choir?
8. Do your parents go to the park every day?
9. Do you play cards with your friends?

Page 75 Exercise D

Listen and choose the correct response.

Ex. What do Patty and Peter do during the week?

1. When do you watch your favorite TV program?
2. Why do you eat Italian food?
3. Does Carlos visit his grandparents in Puerto Rico?
4. What kind of books do you like?
5. Where do your nephews live?

Page 77 Exercise C

Listen and put a check under the correct picture.

1. How often do you read them?
2. I call her every day.
3. I don't like him.
4. I wash it every weekend.
5. He calls us all the time.
6. I say "hello" to them every morning.

Page 78 Exercise G

Listen and choose the correct answer.

1. Henry's car is always very dirty.
2. My husband sometimes makes dinner.
3. My neighbors play loud music at night.
4. My grandparents rarely speak English.
5. Jane always spends a lot of time with her friends.
6. I rarely study in the library.

Page 82 Exercise N

Listen and choose the correct response.

1. Do you have curly hair?
2. Are you married?
3. Does he have brown eyes?
4. Do you have a brother?
5. Do you usually go out on weekends?
6. Is your husband heavy?
7. Do you live in the city?
8. Do you have short hair?

Page 89 Exercise H

As you listen to each story, read the sentences and check yes or no.

Jennifer and Jason

Jennifer and Jason are visiting their grandfather in California. They're sad today. Their grandfather usually takes them to the park, but he isn't taking them to the park today.

Our Boss

Our boss usually smiles at the office, but he isn't smiling today. He's upset because the people in our office aren't working very hard today. It's Friday, and everybody is thinking about the weekend.

On Vacation

When my family and I are on vacation, I always have a good time. I usually play tennis, but when it's cold, I play games on my computer and watch videos. Today is a beautiful day, and I'm swimming at the beach.

Timmy and His Brother

Timmy and his brother are watching a science fiction movie. Timmy is covering his eyes because he's scared. He doesn't like science fiction movies. Timmy's brother isn't scared. He likes science fiction movies.

Page 91 Exercise E

Listen and choose the correct response.

Ex. What are Peter and Tom doing today?

1. What do mail carriers do every day?
2. Where are you going today?
3. What do you do when you're scared?
4. Do you usually use a typewriter?
5. Where do you usually study?

Page 93 Exercise D

Listen and circle the word you hear.

1. Our teacher can speak French.
2. I can't play the piano.
3. He can paint houses.
4. My sister can play soccer.
5. They can't sing.
6. Can you drive a bus?

7. I can't read Japanese newspapers.
8. My son Tommy can play the drums.
9. Their children can't swim.
10. Can your husband cook?
11. We can't skate.
12. I can use a cash register.

Page 97 Exercise K

Listen and circle the words you hear.

1. We have to go to the supermarket.
2. My son has to play his violin every day.
3. We can use business software on our computers.
4. Boris has to speak English every day now.
5. I can't cook Italian food.
6. Apartment building superintendents have to repair locks and paint apartments.
7. That actress can't act!
8. Our children have to use a computer to do their homework.
9. Mr. Johnson can operate equipment.

Page 98 Exercise M

Listen and choose the correct answer.

1. I'm sorry. I can't go to the movies with you today. I have to go to the dentist.
2. I can't go to the party on Saturday. I have to wash my clothes.
3. I can't have lunch with you, but I can have dinner.
4. We can't go skiing this weekend. We have to paint our kitchen.
5. I'm very busy today. I have to go shopping, and I have to cook dinner for my family.
6. I can't see a play with you on Friday because I have to baby-sit. But I can see a play with you on Saturday.

Page 102 Exercise H

Listen and circle the words you hear.

1. I'm going to visit her this year.
2. I'm going to write to my uncle right away.
3. I'm going to call them this Monday.
4. When are you going to cut your hair?
5. I'm going to fix it next Tuesday.
6. We're going to see them this December.
7. They're going to visit us this winter.
8. I'm going to clean it at once.
9. We're going to spend time with them this August.
10. I'm going to wash them immediately.
11. You're going to see us next week.
12. When are you going to call the plumber?

Page 103 Exercise J

Listen to the following weather forecasts and circle the correct answers.

Today's Weather Forecast

This is Mike Martinez with today's weather forecast. This afternoon it's going to be cool and cloudy, with temperatures from 50 to 55 degrees Fahrenheit. This evening it's going to be foggy and warm, but it isn't going to rain.

This Weekend's Weather Forecast

This is Barbara Burrows with your weekend weather forecast. Tonight it's going to be clear and warm, with 60 degree temperatures. On Saturday you can swim at the beach. It's going to be sunny and very hot, with temperatures between 90 and 95 degrees Fahrenheit. But take your umbrella with you on Sunday because it's going to be cool and it's going to rain.

Monday's Weather Forecast

This is Al Alberts with Monday's weather forecast. Monday morning it's going to be cool and nice, but Monday afternoon wear your gloves and your boots because it's going to be very cold and it's going to snow! On Tuesday morning the skiing is going to be wonderful because it's going to be sunny and very warm!

Page 108 Exercise T

Listen and write the time you hear.

1. It's seven forty-five.
2. It's six fifteen.
3. It's four thirty.
4. It's nine fifteen.
5. It's midnight.
6. It's five o'clock.
7. It's a quarter to nine.
8. It's a quarter after eight.
9. It's one forty-five.
10. It's noon.
11. It's eleven thirty.
12. It's a quarter to three.

Page 113 Exercise G

Listen to the story. Fill in the correct times.

Every day at school I study English, science, mathematics, music, and Chinese. English class begins at 8:30. I go to science at 10:15 and mathematics at 11:00. We have lunch at 12:15. We go to music at 12:45, and we have Chinese at 1:30.

Page 114 Exercise B

Listen to the story. Put the number under the correct picture.

Everybody in my family is sick today.

My parents are sick.
1. My father has a stomachache.
2. My mother has a backache.

My brother and my sister are sick, too.
3. My sister Alice has an earache.
4. My brother David has a toothache.

My grandparents are also sick.
5. My grandmother has a cold.
6. My grandfather has a sore throat.
7. Even my dog is sick! He has a fever!

Yes, everybody in my family is sick today . . . everybody except me!

How do I feel today?
8. I feel fine!

Page 117 Exercise F

Listen and circle the correct answer.

Example 1: I study.
Example 2: I played cards.

1. I planted flowers.
2. I shave.
5. I work.
6. I shouted.
7. I clean.
8. I studied.
3. I cried.
4. I typed.
9. I fixed my car.
10. I paint.
11. I smile.
12. I cooked.

Page 126 Exercise I

Listen and choose the correct response.

1. When did you write to your girlfriend?
2. When does your neighbor wash his car?
3. Who did your parents visit?
4. Where does Irene do yoga?
5. When did your son go to sleep?
6. When do you clean your apartment?
7. Where did you take your grandchildren?
8. What did you make for dinner?
9. When does Carla read her e-mail?
10. When did you get up today?

Page 129 Exercise B

Listen and circle the word you hear.

1. My husband is thin.
2. She was very hungry.
3. They were tired today.
4. He was very energetic at school today.
5. My wife is at the clinic.
6. Their clothes were clean.
7. My children are very sick today.
8. My parents are home tonight.
9. He was very full this morning.
10. The Lopez family is on vacation.
11. Their neighbors are very noisy.
12. These clothes were dirty.

Page 131 Exercise E

Listen and circle the word you hear.

1. I wasn't busy yesterday.
2. We were at the movies last night.
3. They weren't home today.
4. Tom was on time for his plane.
5. It wasn't cold yesterday.
6. They weren't at the baseball game.
7. My friends were late for the party.
8. The doctor was in her office at noon.

Page 134 Exercise I

Listen and choose the correct response.

1. Where were you born?
2. Where did you grow up?
3. What was your favorite subject in school?
4. When did you move here?
5. What did you look like when you were young?
6. Did you have freckles?
7. What do you do in your spare time?
8. Did you have a favorite hero?

Page 137 Exercise F

Listen and circle the word you hear.

Ex. Is Jane rich or poor?

1. It was a nice day today.
2. My friends were thirsty at lunch.
3. Who is your favorite hero?
4. Were Mr. and Mrs. Parker at home last weekend?
5. My new couch is uncomfortable.
6. My cousins were late for their plane.
7. Before I met Howard, I was very sad.
8. Your children are very cute.

Correlation Key

Student Book Pages	Activity Workbook Pages	Student Book Pages	Activity Workbook Pages
Chapter 9		**Chapter 15**	
80	62–63 Exercises A, B	142	114–115
81	63 Exercise C–66	143	116–117
82	67–68	144–145	118–121
Chapter 10		**Chapter 16**	
88	69	150	122–123
89	70–71	151	124–125
90–91	72–73	152	126
95	74	153	127–128
Check-Up Test	75	**Chapter 17**	
Chapter 11		158	129
100	76–77	159	130
101	78–79	160	131
102	80	161	132–133
103	81–82	163	134–135
Chapter 12		Check-Up Test	136–137
108–109	83–86		
110–111	87–90		
Check-Up Test	91		
Chapter 13			
118	92–93 Exercise B		
119	93 Exercise C–95		
122	96–97		
123	98–99		
Chapter 14			
128	100		
129	101		
130–131	102–103 Exercise I		
133	103 Exercise J–107		
134–135	108–111		
Check-Up Test	112–113		